MW00824086

Greek Life

family | culture | food

EUGENIA PANTAHOS

Published in 2014 by Greek Lifestyle

National Library of Australia Cataloguing-in-Publication entry
Author: Pantahos, Eugenia
Title: Greek Life: family, culture, food Eugenia Pantahos
ISBN: 9780992515300 (hardback)
Subjects: Cooking, Greek
Families--Greek
Greeks--Social life and customs
Dewey Number: 641.59495

Selected Photography: Zoe Coates
Design Concept: Steve Grice
Printed by PWGS, Singapore.
Soft Cover published 2016

COOKING NOTES

Cooking times may vary depending on the oven you are using.
250ml cup used for measurement

www.greeklifestyle.com.au

σας καλωσορίζω

Welcome

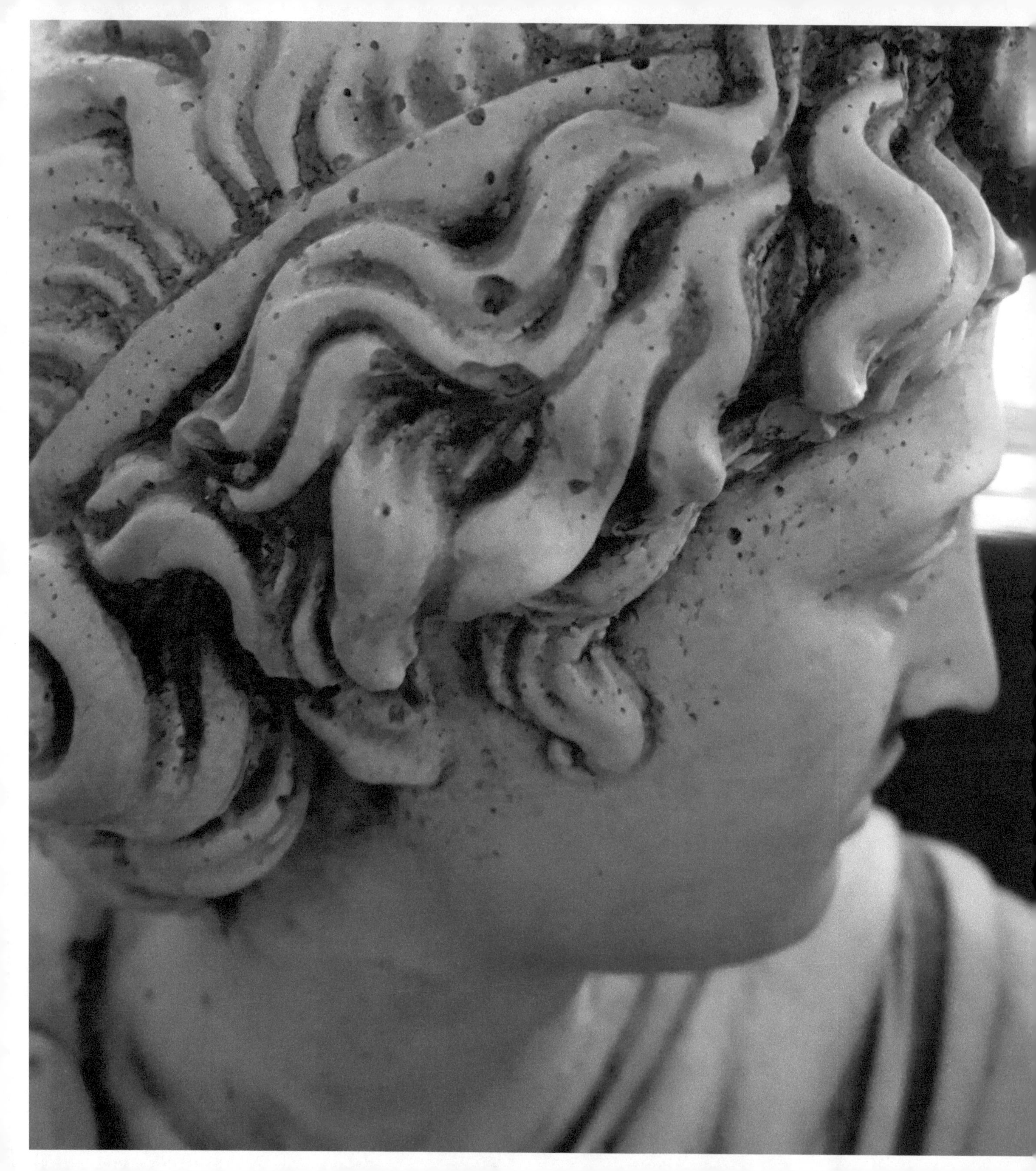

EUGENIA PANTAHOS

www.greeklifestyle.com.au

SELECTED STYLING AND PHOTOGRAPHY BY EUGENIA PANTAHOS

ESTD
1850
N.G.CALLICOUNIS
DISTILLERIES
OUZO
XENIA
OUZO
ΜΥΤΙΛΗΝΗΣ
O IZO
of
plomari
Isidoros Arvanitis
Μακρινίτσα

Contents

The Story of Family 021

The Greek Calendar 037

Love and Other Ceremonies 127

Births and Baptisms 149

Death and Mourning 161

Entertaining 185

Kitchen and Garden 203

Greek Way of Life 251

This book is dedicated lovingly to my three daughters, Anna, Mary and Helena.

Know where you came from so that you may know where you are heading.

Embrace the lessons shared, be authentic and always stay true to yourself.

φιλοσοφια

Philosophy

“Knowing yourself is the beginning of all wisdom.”

Aristotle

Introduction

This book came out of a desire to create an historical family memoir and to pass forward the teachings of my parents, John and Maria Desyllas, about our beautiful and meaningful Greek customs and traditions.

Many hours have been spent at my computer taking my handwritten notes and personal memories and turning them into what I see as an invaluable reference book, not just for my immediate family but also for other members of the diaspora (people living elsewhere as a result of their parents or grandparents migrating) and omogenia (those of Greek heritage who have never lived in Greece, and nor have their immediate forebears).

In this book I have not only included wisdom passed on to me by my parents, but also lessons I learned as I travelled through Greece, speaking to relatives, along with lessons from my husband's parents, who have also shared their stories.

This book is a celebration of Hellenism. My intention is to share with readers something of what it means to be Greek, and what it is like to live the unique Greek way of life. The book imparts to both Hellenes (people of Greek origin) and Philhellenes (lovers of Greek culture) just some of the beautiful, rich and symbolic cultural offerings of the Greeks. I say 'some' because each region of Greece has it's own nuances, cultures and special customs.

Greek Life commences at the start of the calendar year and provides information about cultural life, accompanied by authentic regional recipes and traditions, from New Year through to Christmas. The book also explains the cultural practices of other major life events, such as engagements, weddings, baptisms and farewelling our loved ones, along with a sprinkling of thought-provoking Greek philosophy (a little mind food).

My parents taught us first and foremost the meaning of family and unity, of love and guidance, protection and inclusion. Entwined intrinsically with this way of life, is our Orthodox faith.

Family get-togethers are regular and often. We celebrate everything that life offers us. This love of life allows us to live in the present and also prepares us for the difficult times in life; those of loss and mourning. During these solemn times there are special customs to be performed, and memorials practised. Life, as well as death, is honoured and celebrated.

In my family, grandparents are respected elders who share life lessons and wisdom freely. Aunts and uncles, being the second generation, are custodians of the traditions. Members of the third generation pursue their studies and work, raising their young families whilst embracing the traditions. Finally, the fourth generation being the great-grandchildren, enjoy special friendships with family members from each generation. It is a circle of love that is never ending.

I hope you enjoy the journey, and that you will use Greek Life to continue the celebration of the timeless and unique Greek traditions.

Thank you,
Eugenia.

φιλοσοφια

Philosophy

"Wisdom begins in wonder."

Socrates

Not long before my mother passed away, my father had been hospitalized. Mum was in her early eighties and in recent times had become a little frail and less independent. Staying home alone whilst Dad was in hospital was not a real option, so Mum came to stay with me and my family.

This was to be the first and last time that Mum would visit one of her children under extenuating circumstances. Although Mum had visited my sister in Melbourne many times (when her babies were born, to help her family move house, and just regular visits to keep in touch and add her special kind of love and assistance) these trips of loving support for her children were made when she was younger, more vital and full of life.

Mum was initially quite reluctant to come and stay with my family, but it was essential for her own safety and well-being, and for keeping her occupied during this stressful time. I'm happy that she agreed to stay and, after we worked through her uncertainties, we were able to share a treasured and special time together. My siblings came to visit with their families, and they brought their children and grandchildren. Some of us shared a simple lunch together and later, as others arrived, we sat in the back garden soaking in the afternoon sun, sipping tea and enjoying cake. The great-grand children doted on their great-grandmother and made sure she felt very loved and cared for. Their energy and chatter was uplifting and a welcome distraction.

The following afternoon Mum and I were in our sitting room having coffee and watching the end of a Parios music concert. I took the opportunity to mention the idea for this book, switched on my computer and showed her my first draft.

She loved it, saying Tin Efhi mou na ehis : "I give you my blessing". Then she tilted her head to one side and looked at me lovingly. Cheekily, she said, "You were listening to me".

Mum was excited and genuinely proud. When she began reciting love and other quotes, I quickly put my fingers into action and started typing. It is an afternoon that will stay with me forever, and I feel blessed to have shared the idea for this book with my mother because now it is infused not only with her love, her lessons and her spirit, but also with her blessing. That is something every child values, and I will appreciate it until the end of time. Sadly and unexpectedly my mother passed away one month later, and she shall always be so very deeply missed.

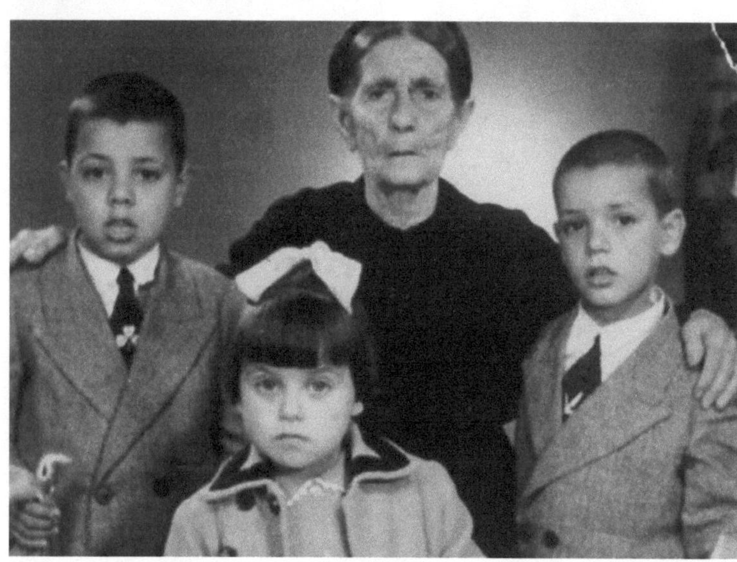

The Story of Family

The Beginning

My parents were born in the village of Skourohorion, in Pyrgos Elias, a beautiful part of Greece that enjoys a wonderful Mediterranean climate, located on the western side of the Peloponnesian peninsula. The village is situated on a plain near the Ionian Sea and the landscape is filled with forests, pines, citrus, eucalypts, plane trees, olive groves, farmland and vineyards. Nearby is the capital of Pyrgos (meaning 'tower') and the ancient city of Olympia, the birthplace of the first Olympic Games held in 776BC. Close-by is Katakolon, the seaside town that welcomes magnificent cruise ships into its port, and the beautiful Aghios Andreas beach with it's stunning crystal-clear water that makes for perfect swimming.

Dad's father, Kosta, was born in 1892 on the island of Zakynthos, one of the seven islands of the Ionian Sea known as eptanisia ('seven islands'). Pappou Kosta served in World War One, then migrated to the Peloponnese, making Skourohori his home. In 1922, aged 30, he married my yiayia Lambrini and went on to have seven children, the third of which was my father.

Pappou Kosta owned the Pantopoleion, the shop in the village square, as well as farmland. My grandparents had two houses; one in the village and the other was their homestead (exohico) built with local stone which was used as a summer house. The smaller buildings on the property were white-washed each spring in readiness for the summer holiday when the family would gather. The homestead was surrounded by a beautiful ornamental herb garden and, along with a well, the property had a vast amount of fig trees, olive groves, raisin vines, and a magnificent mulberry tree with fruit-laden branches hanging low to the ground.

Zakynthians are warm-hearted people, and the melodic intonations with which they speak are well recognised. Remarkably, my siblings and I have inherited this idiosyncratic expressiveness and on a recent visit to Greece an Athenian shopkeeper confidently stated, "I know you are from Zakynthos". You could only imagine my surprise – especially as I was not born in Greece! I questioned his proclamation, to which he replied, "It's simple, you sing when you speak. It's like music". My heritage seems to be with me where ever I go!

My mother's maternal family was originally from Lagkadia, a picturesque township some 48 kilometres east of Olympia, with imposing views and fresh water springs. I am the namesake of my maternal grandmother, yiayia Evyenia, who was married at a young age, widowed for two years, then married my grandfather, Andreas.

Pappou Andreas was an artisan shoemaker and owner of an atelier, the workshop of an artist. They went on to have five children, my mother being the youngest. Pappou Andreas passed away when my mother was only six months old, leaving my grandmother widowed again, with a young family to care for. Fortunately, yiayia Evyenia had a large number of sheep, and many parcels of farmland that were leased to fellow villagers, and this afforded her independence.

During the war the Italian invading forces commandeered yiayia's home and used it as their headquarters. Their demands had to be abided and my grandmother was forced to rent a small house in the village, surrendering her home with all its supplies, including home-prepared olives, olive oil, feta, wine, and much more.

In the warmer months the family moved back to their farming property and into the homestead (exohico), where the surrounding trees made the climate cooler. It also meant that yiayia could save paying rent while being better able to manage the sheep and land leases.

Although the landscape surrounding Pyrgos Elias provided plentiful harvests, the war years were difficult and many people died from starvation. The long days were filled with hard work; tending crops and stock, trying to make ends meet, with the family doing the best they could during these times of frugality. It was waste not, want not, and often times a loaf of homemade bread was the only sustenance shared between the entire family. School was sacrificed and opportunities were cut short. Each family member had their place and knew that their contribution was needed if the family was to survive.

As young teenagers after the war, my mother and father had fallen in love. During this time my father worked for his family, managing the family shop in the plaka ('village square'), working the farmland, raising livestock, tending to their raisin vines and harvesting the fruit for sale. My mother managed her family household too, at one time nursing her own mother through a terminal illness. But with her blessing, my parents married as soon as they could, which was fifteen months after yiayia's passing, respectfully observing a one year mourning period, then the forty days of lent leading up to Christmas, when weddings were not allowed. Their love could wait no longer than that, so they were married the day after Christmas, 1951, with their first child born in November, 1952.

My mother's family home was located near St. Spyridon church, and my mother felt a deep connection with this Saint, who is celebrated on 12th December. Mum chose St. Spyridon as her patron saint and she prayed to him, counted her blessings with him, and felt that he guided her throughout her life. My mother would say, "proskinao tin hari to Aghiou Spyridonas", which translates to "I worship the blessing of St. Spyridon", and she believed that her beloved Saint was instrumental in bestowing the blessings she experienced.

Along with the rest of the world, Greece had endured many hardships throughout World War Two, and shortly after, in 1946, Greece descended into civil war. The country was in turmoil and thousands fled. Four years into their marriage, now with three small children, the youngest only three months, my parents looked for a future elsewhere.

After World War Two the Australian Government promoted the policy known as 'Populate or Perish', to help increase the population of Australia. People came from all over Europe and during the next few years hundreds of Greek migrants arrived in Australia. In 1953 the Greek Assisted Passage Agreement was put into place with many Greek nationals, including my mother's brother arriving in Australia over coming years. My father's journey was a sponsored passage whereby my mother's brother issued an invitation to my father; and so the journey began. My parents' decision was not made lightly, for it meant giving up everything that was familiar; language, culture, family, friends and the traditional Greek way of life. But it also meant the promise of the family being able to prosper elsewhere.

I still cannot comprehend the depth of sacrifice made by our parents, and the many others who made the same decision. What I do know is that I am thankful for the opportunities afforded to me because of their choice.

Dad made provisions to ensure that Mum and his three children had security while he was away. He commissioned and helped with the building of a humble home that he only enjoyed with his young family for a short period of time.

On St. Spyridon's Day, the 12th of December 1955, the family farewelled my Dad at the village station, bound ultimately for Australia. Just before Dad boarded the train, with his clothes and belongings in a simple bundle under his arm, his mother said:

Τα ξενα θελουνε οιπομονι,
Θελουν καπινοσινι
Θελουν λαγου περπατιμα,
μετα θελουν αετο γριγοσινι.

A foreign land requires patience,
It requires hard work.
Walk like a hare, head down, and staying alert,
Be as quick as an eagle to return home.

Ancient Greece was the home to philosophers who shaped the world we live in; the teachings and wisdom of Plato, Socrates, Aristotle and Epicurus are still taught and embraced today.

φιλοσοφια

Philosophy

"Love is composed of a single soul inhabiting two bodies."

Aristotle

Dad spent the next few days in Athens, living with Mum's brother whilst he completed the necessary paperwork and attended appointments at the Immigration Department. With a suitcase given to him by his cousin, Dad left Greece on the 17th of December, 1955, upon the ship Flaminia departing from the Port of Pireaus, to take the twenty six day journey to Australia.

Sailing on the Aegean waters and through the Suez Canal, the ship eventually docked at Fremantle, just long enough for the passengers to have a quick look around. The Flaminia then made its way to Melbourne, arriving on the 15th of January, 1956. Dad stayed in Melbourne overnight and on the following evening caught the overnight train to Adelaide. He started work the very next day, and for the next two years Australia was to be his home.

My father worked very hard. He spent three weeks working in Adelaide, one month harvesting fruit in Mildura, then four years on the railways; two at Red Hill and two at Manoora. Every February Dad took four weeks off from work, two weeks as annual leave and two weeks of unpaid leave, so that he could spend a full month harvesting fruit at Mildura. He did this for five consecutive years, saving diligently to support his family and working towards buying a house in Australia.

Being so far away from home, Dad experienced great loneliness and isolation. However he had a dream for his family and knew that the sacrifice was worthwhile. Regardless of how difficult his circumstances were, having the opportunity to make choices was very important to Dad. This freedom allowed Dad to better the future of his children, even though it involved him making the transition from being a land and business owner to a worker on the railways, and later in a factory. My father was fearless. He considered that as long as he was able to work, then everything was possible. Dad could see that Australia was indeed full of opportunity and that the future of his family would be more secure here.

My parents made tremendous sacrifices during this time of separation. Two years quickly became three, four, five and then six. My eldest siblings lived without their father for six years, our mother taking on the role of both parents. My mother's much beloved Aunt Vasilliki, her father's sister, moved in with Mum to offer company, support, comfort, and especially love and guidance during this very difficult time.

My parents kept in touch by letter, and exchanged them regularly. As a small child I remember going into my mother's bedroom and opening the bottom drawer of her dressing table to find it filled to the brim with handwritten letters. The envelopes were made of a thin, blueish paper with a blue and white border, and striking Greek stamps on the right hand corner. Sometimes I opened the letters to have a little look, but at six years of age with a limited ability to read Greek, I really couldn't understand too much.

There was another suitcase in the old shed with more letters – six years worth! Six years of Mum and Dad's lives recorded with pen and paper, sent by ship, each taking weeks to arrive. I can only imagine the great joy they must have felt in their hearts when each letter was received, and how much each one would have meant.

With his hard work and very little personal expenses, Dad was able to send money back home to support his family. He saved very diligently and bought his first property in Australia in 1960. The property would become a true family home, and is still our patriarchal home today – one that is special in our hearts, and where we have made many family memories.

In 1961, arrangements were made for Mum and my three eldest siblings to prepare for their journey to Australia. Mum packed her belongings and some of her beautiful possessions, and farewelled her brothers and their families, her friends and her beloved Aunt. With a Greek-English dictionary in hand she firmly resolved to learn some of the language on her journey to Australia. This in itself shows just how determined my mother was. Her strength of character and willingness to learn is inspirational, and is something that she pursued and exemplified all her life. At Pireaus, the family of four boarded the ship Patris, which means 'homeland' in Greek, to sail on the Aegean Sea and through the Suez Canal, following the same course as my father's ship in 1955.

Mum and my three eldest siblings arrived in Australia in 1961, some six years after Dad had left Greece. My siblings initially felt their father a stranger to them, until the distance of time was slowly bridged with Mum's tremendous assistance. Mum was a dynamic and strong lady who withstood and endured hardships with dignity and tenacity. She had held her family close, cared for them lovingly, and with absolute dedication would bring them all together again. With the loving couple reunited at last, a fourth child arrived within a year, in April 1962. We refer to our sister as 'the love child'. Within two years I came along, completing the family of seven.

My parents were totally devoted to each other, and their family was most precious to them both. They dedicated their lives to all of us, ensuring that our needs were met, our spirits developed, our souls nourished and that we all possessed the valuable life skills we required to move forward with upward momentum. As a result, many philosophical conversations occurred around the kitchen table. Meal times were an opportunity to share stories, to help us understand hardship, hopes, dreams, unity and love.

I'd like to share a valuable piece of wisdom imparted to me by my father that subtly sums up the collective traits required to not only survive life's hardships, but to endure and flourish.

Greek Proverb

Ο καλός καραβοκύρης
στη φουρτούνα φαίνεται.

The ability of a sea captain
Is only evident in the storm.

My parents embraced Australia as their new home. They maintained a delicate balance; holding onto their heritage, whilst assimilating into their new community. Lifelong relationships were formed with their neighbors, who had greatly assisted Mum and Dad with paperwork, medical appointments and know-how in their early years here, and my parents remained eternally grateful for the kind support shown to them.

An important day for my parents was when they became naturalized as Australian citizens. We all wore our best outfits and headed to our local council for the ceremony. We knew that this was a special day and we needed to be on our best behavior. I was only quite young, however I remember admiring my parents and thinking just how beautiful and elegant my mother looked. Mum and Dad proudly came home with their citizenship certificates, and we still have the family photo taken after the ceremony.

My parents committed many years to building and nurturing their family. Dad worked very hard during the day, and attended to his garden in the early morning and late afternoon. Mum spent hours sewing our dresses and coats, knitting jumpers and cardigans, and crocheting ponchos and pinafores. During the colder months her knitting needles worked quickly to knit our new winter jumpers and cardigans. When we had outgrown our outfits Mum would unravel the yarn, and it was our job to roll it up into a ball for future use. Yarn was never wasted, it would be re-used to knit warm and comfortable bed socks. Often when we arrived home after school, we would also find Mum busy sewing. The Singer sewing machine was housed in the enclosed sunny back verandah, which was a wonderful source of natural light. Mum worked tirelessly for her family, and we remember with much fondness the love and dedication that she put into everything she did.

At home my mother spent many hours working in her kitchen preparing traditional meals, lovingly cooked using many ingredients harvested from the garden that my father expertly tended. When arriving home, mouthwatering aromas of baked rice-stuffed tomatoes, manestra soup, lemon and oregano roasted lamb, or fish frying in the pan would welcome us. More often than not there would also be a serving tray waiting, with small bowls of freshly made creamy rizogalo (rice pudding) sprinkled with nutmeg or cinnamon, protectively covered by a fresh linen tea towel.

φιλοσοφια

Philosophy

"Hope is a waking dream."

Aristotle

My mother always loved her plants and after I, the youngest of the children, had started school she found a little more time for nurturing an ornamental garden. She slowly filled it with flowers; stunning roses and camellias, beautifully perfumed carnations, and impatiens in a variety of colours, both double and single flowers. There were also gardenias, cosmos, ferns, succulents, orchids and palms, just to name a few. Mum also grew traditional Greek herbs, not just for cooking but for medicinal and ornamental value. However, Mum's most prized and loved plants were begonias, in both the small form and large tree varieties, single bloom and double bloom, and also fairy-winged. She simply loved them, and I love nurturing the plants that she gave to me as little cuttings that have now become large specimens with beautiful blooms. They take pride of place outside my back door, under the verandah where I can admire them daily.

I remember attending my school fete when I was five years old and, with some small change in my pocket, trying to choose a plant to buy for my mother. I looked carefully at what was on offer. There were lots of succulents and most of them had thorns, and I wasn't fond of these. I then saw a lovely succulent that looked like a rose flower. It was called Haworthia, and I chose this pretty little succulent for my Mum, and took it home very proudly. To this day, some 44 years later, my parents' garden still features several pots of Haworthia. My mother-in-law also has a pot, I have several, and of course over this period of time many friends and family have received little shoots to take home with them too.

Mum very proudly tended and admired her ornamental garden, and her dedication and work was enjoyed by taking strolls and perhaps a cup of coffee with Dad in either of the two courtyards that she designed. During the summer months my parents enjoyed sitting on the front verandah overlooking the ornamental garden whilst partaking in some freshly cut watermelon, figs from their tree, or the old-fashioned, small sultana grapes, harvested from their vine.

Maintaining links to Greek culture was also extremely important to Mum and Dad, and in 1972 the Elion Society 'Olympic Flame' of South Australia was formed.

The Elion Society celebrates the birthplace of the Olympic Games, and each year at the annual dance there is a reenactment of the lighting of the Olympic flame, complete with the young runner boy bearing the lit torch and young girls dressed in the traditional Olympic-style dresses, performing classic Greek dances. My sisters and I participated in this event many years ago, as did our own daughters and nieces, and now we all get to admire the great-grandchildren of the family continuing this wonderful, historic and meaningful celebration of Hellenic culture.

In many ways my mother was a pioneer. She became the first female committee member of the Elion Society, and she also served on the ladies committee for many years. My father was one of the original founders of the club. He has now been a volunteer at the Elion Society for over 40 consecutive years, tirelessly giving his time, energy and passion to a society that he deeply cares about, as do we.

My parents made great sacrifices to become proud parents of a large family. After we all married, Mum and Dad spent some wonderful times holidaying both within Australia, and of course in Greece, with extensive travels through Europe and the USA. This was their time, a time to catch up on the lost years.

Mum and Dad enjoyed a life of love, passion and unity – something we all deeply admire. My father lovingly penned the poem below in a moment of deep inspiration and continued love for my mother.

Η Μαρία με το θησαυρό

Εχασα την γηναικα μου
Στα 82 της τα χρονια
Αλλα μου αφισε ενα θησαυρό
Για αυτο και ζω ακομα

Την βλεπω παντα διπλα μου
Εκι που περπαταω
Δεν την ξεχάσα ποτε
Γιατη την αγαπαω

Γιαννις - 7 Μαιι 2014

Maria's treasure

I lost my wife
When she was 82
She left me with a treasure of familial wealth
And for that reason, I live.

I see her beside me always
Wherever it is that I walk
I will never forget her
Because I love her

Yiannis - 7 May 2014

Greece is the jewel of Europe, where east meets west, standing between the sparkling waters of the Aegean and Ionian Seas – proudly revered as both "The Cradle of Western Civilization" and "The Birthplace of Democracy", home to the genesis of The Olympic Games, and the origins of drama, literature, science and mathematical principles.

φιλοσοφια

Philosophy

"One minute of patience, ten years of peace."

Greek Proverb

The Greek Calendar

The New Year

January brings with it the start of the New Year, and is an ideal time for families to come together and celebrate as the clock ticks past midnight. It is also a time for reflection, renewal and revival, a time for embracing one's life, appreciating those around us, and sharing love and happiness. It is a time for new beginnings, new hopes, new dreams, new plans – and new shoes!

Celebrations commence on New Year's Eve, and this may take place by attending a dinner, a dance, a ball or an informal gathering. Important to any Greek celebration is lots of delicious food, good company and of course dancing. Opa!

New Year's Day is the feast day of St. Basil (Aghios Vassilios), the Greek equivalent of Santa Claus, and he is honoured on this day. On New Year's Day, those named Vassilios and Vassiliki celebrate their name day.

St. Basil was one the forefathers of the Greek Orthodox Church and he is remembered for his generosity to the poor and his kindness to children. The story has it that he would come in the night and leave gifts for the children, placing them in their shoes. In times gone by, New Year's Day was traditionally the main day for exchanging gifts, and this makes it an even more festive occasion than Christmas. Today, however, as is usual around the world, gift giving occurs at Christmas time.

At the stroke of midnight on New Year's Eve, family and friends gather around closely. The lights are dimmed, the count down is on and anticipation prevails. Greetings are exchanged with kisses on both cheeks and wishes for "Hronia Polla" ("Happy Years") or "Kalee Hronia" ("Have a Good Year").

At midnight the folk song O Aghios Vasslis Erherta ("St. Basil Is Arriving") is sung. St. Basil, dressed like Father Christmas, walks among the people tossing wrapped sweets into the crowd. Eager children and adults scurry to pick up the sweets, and the excitement continues with good humour.

After midnight, in the early hours of the morning, we all gather at home for delicious loukoumades (donoughts drizzled in honey and cinnamon). A foil-wrapped coin is placed into the batter at the time of cooking and, once served, the person who finds the coin in their loukoumades is believed to have good fortune for the remainder of the year. One needs to be a little cautious before biting into the loukoumades. It is best done gently and deliberately to preserve one's teeth!

The Vassilopita (bread of St. Basil) is also served, and this too has a foil-wrapped coin inside. The family gathers at the dinner table and traditionally the father, as the head of the family, makes a sign of the cross over the bread three times. The bread is then cut into slices. The first piece is cut in honour of the home and then a piece is sliced for each family member, addressed by name, starting with the most senior member of the household and slicing down to the youngest member, including any absent family members. The family eagerly partakes in the Vassiloptita in search of the lucky coin, and to see who will have good fortune for the year ahead.

It is a tradition for Greek families to play card games on New Year's Eve as they like to participate in games of chance, and hope for good luck to come their way. Many people enjoy staying up all night with their family and friends waiting to see the new day dawn whilst enjoying the delicious loukoumades, vassilopita and the fun of playing card games.

An important tradition observed on New Year's Day revolves around the significance attached to the first person crossing the threshold of the home. With greetings of "Hronia Polla", the person must enter the home stepping with the right foot first, as it is believed that this person will bring good fortune into the home for the coming year. Often a child is the preferred first guest for this special practice because children are considered innocent and their hearts free of malice and envy.

Traditional Greek New Years Song

Ayios Vasilis erhete
Ke den mas katadehete
Apo, apo tin kesaria.
Sis arhon sis arhondissa Kiria!
Vastari penna ke harti
Zaharokandio zimoni
Harti, harti ke kalamari
Des eme, des eme, to pallikari!

To kalamari egrafe
Ti mira toy tin elege
Ke to, ke to harti omili.
To hriso, to hriso mas kaiofili!

Arhiminia kiarhihronia
Psili mou dendrolivania,
Ke arhi, ke arhi kalos mas hronos.
Eklisia, eklisia, me tayio thronos!

Arhi pou vgiken o Hristos
Ayios ke Pnevmatikos,
Sti gi, gi na perpatisi
Ke na mas, ke na mas kalokardisi!

English Translation

Saint Basil comes,
And does not acknowledge us
From Caesarea.
You are, you are the mistress of the house!

He holds a pen and paper
And leavened sweets
Paper, paper and ink. Look at me, look at me, the brave one!

The ink wrote
And told fortunes,
And the, and the paper spoke.
Our golden, our golden clove!

It is the first day of the month and the year,
My tall rosemary,
And from, and from the beginning a good year for us.
The church, the church with the holy throne!

Christ came in the beginning,
Holy and Spiritual;
On earth, on earth he walked
To give us, to give us good cheer!

Vasilopita
New Year Bread

Ingredients

1 cup warm milk [use 1/2 to dissolve the yeast]

2 teaspoons yeast

3 eggs, beaten

1 cup butter, melted

1 1/2 cups caster sugar

2 crystals of mahlepi, crushed with 1 teaspoon of sugar

Zest of 1 lemon or orange

1 level teaspoon salt

1 kilo plain fine flour

1 coin wrapped in foil

Glaze and Topping

1 egg and 1 teaspoon of water, mixed

Handful of blanched almonds (to decorate)

Method

Preheat oven to 180c

Beat together the eggs, caster sugar and citrus.

In a large tub sift the flour, salt and ground mahlepi, and make a well in the centre.

Dissolve the yeast in 1/2 a cup of the warm milk. Add the yeast to the flour mixture and stir to blend in the flour, gradually adding the warm melted butter and beaten eggs.

Knead for approximately 10 minutes or until the dough is smooth and elastic.

Place the ball of dough into a clean bowl brushed with melted butter, and turn the dough over to brush the other side. Cover with a clean tea towel and let the dough rise in a warm place until it has doubled in size.

Knead the dough for 5 minutes more and place in a large round, oiled pan, and leave covered in a warm place until it doubles in size again.

Before placing in the oven, insert the foil-covered coin, beat the reserved egg yolk with a teaspoon of water and brush it over the dough with a pastry brush to glaze the top.

Using the blanched almonds, arrange them to form the date of the new year on the top of the dough.

Bake for about 30-45 minutes, or until golden brown.

If the bread browns too quickly, place a piece of aluminum foil on top. Cool on a wire rack.

Vasilopita

Easy New Year Cake

Ingredients

4 cups plain flour, sifted

6 teaspoons baking powder

1 teaspoon salt

1 cup butter

1 1/2 cups sugar

4 eggs

1 1/2 cups milk

Grated orange or lemon rind

1/4 cup cognac or brandy [optional]

Icing sugar for dusting when serving

Method

Sift together the flour, baking powder and salt.

Cream the butter, and gradually add the sugar, beating together until the mixture is light and fluffy.

Add the eggs, one at a time, beating well after each addition.

Add the flour and milk alternatively, and mix well.

Add the lemon rind and cognac, if used.

Grease a 12-inch round baking pan and line with baking paper.

Place batter into the pan, and put a foil wrapped coin into the mixture.

Bake for approximately 40 minutes.

Allow the cake to cool.

Turn out onto serving plate, dust with icing sugar and serve.

Loukoumathes

Honey Donoughts

Ingredients

1 tablespoon dry yeast

1 cup warm milk

1/4 cup warm water
(more if necessary)

2 tablespoons sugar

1 1/2 cups plain flour

pinch of salt

Sunflower oil for
deep-frying

Honey, warmed slowly in a
small stainless steel pot

Ground cinnamon for
dusting and serving

Method

Dissolve yeast in 1/4 cup of warm milk, add 1/2 teaspoon of sugar and allow to double in size.

In a large bowl, sift the remaining flour, salt and sugar.

Add the yeast mixture to the flour. Then add the remainder of the warm milk.

Continue mixing the batter and add warm water as necessary, until a smooth and stringy consistency is reached.

Cover and leave the mixture in a warm place to let rise until doubled.

Pour a little sunflower oil into a small demitasse cup, ready for the frying aprocess.

Heat the oil in a deep frying pan.

To test if the oil is hot enough, drop a small ball of batter into the oil .If the batter expands and quickly rises to the surface, the oil is ready.

When the oil is hot, take a handful of the batter and gently squeeze between the thumb and fingers to make a small ball. Using a long-handed teaspoon that has been dipped in the small demitasse cup of sunflower oil, gently drop the batter into the hot oil.

Fry 5-10 small spoonfuls at a time, dipping the spoon into the oil as required to prevent the batter from sticking. Reduce the heat as required to prevent over-browning.

Fry over moderately slow heat until the batter is puffed and golden brown.

Remove with a slotted spoon and place into a bowl lined with absorbent paper. Toss gently to remove the excess oil.

Place the honey puffs into individual serving bowls, drizzle with warm honey and sprinkle with cinnamon.

HERE
AT HOLDFAST BAY
LANDED THE
PIONEER SETTLERS
AND

January 5th

Eve of Epiphany

This is the Eve of Epiphany (the baptism of Christ) and Greek families will contact their local priest to visit the family home and bestow blessings on the house and those who live there. The priest will come with a bottle of holy water and proceed to bless the house room by room whilst reciting prayers. It is customary to offer a small donation to the church as a gesture of gratitude.

The 5th of January is also the usual day for Christmas decorations to be taken down. The exception to this rule applies to those families who have a household member celebrating their name day on the 7th of January, the day of St. John. Christmas decorations are kept on display whilst those celebrating receive visitors. This allows the festive season to continue for a little longer. Decorations are eventually taken down and packed away on the 8th of January.

January 6th

On 6th January, the Great Feast called Theophany, and the enlightenment called the Epiphany, otherwise known as To Photon, are celebrated. The term Epiphany is known as 'seeing the light' and is a significant term in everyday use. This day is the culmination of the Christmas period and commemorates the baptism of Jesus in the Jordan River by the Prophet John, and marks the Great Blessing of Water. This is the name day for those named Photios, Photini, Jordan or Jordana and celebrations will be enjoyed with family and friends.

A church service is held on the day of the Theophany, even if it falls on a weekday. Attendees take either small glass bottles or jars, or specially designed Agiasmos (Holy Water) bottles with them to church, and at the end of this special service the bottles are filled with sanctified water to take home with them. The holy water is used to bless their homes, gardens and other possessions.

On rising the following morning and before breakfast, it is customary to take a teaspoon of this holy water as a personal blessing. Some households preserve it for the entire year, partaking of it only at times of illness, challenge or personal and family adversity.

On the following Sunday, Orthodox priests and followers congregate at the seaside and read prayers to bless the waters. A crucifix is thrown into the sea, and young divers attempt to prove their worth by trying to be the first to find it. It is considered that good fortune will be bestowed upon the diver who retrieves the crucifix.

Orthodox priests use this sanctified water at baptisms, and also for conducting blessings throughout the year at homes, businesses, schools, tavernas, restaurants, olive groves, gardens, and even on fishing boats. The priest dips a fresh bunch of basil into the holy water, and then using the bunch of basil he proceeds to sprinkle the sweetly scented holy water onto the congregation.

Basil has religious significance because it is believed that the herb was found by Helen, the mother of Constantine the Great, growing beside the cross of Jesus. It is known as 'The King of Herbs', its name derived from the Greek word Basileus meaning 'King'.

January 7th
Feast Day for St John

January 7th is the feast day of St. John, and those named John, Yiannis, Yiannoula or Yanna, will celebrate their name day today. For those celebrating their name day on this day, Christmas trees and decorations will usually be kept up to receive guests and visitors into a festive, decorated home, and then taken down on the 8th of January.

My father's name is John, so from an early age I knew only too well that our Christmas decorations needed to be kept up until after we celebrated Dad's name day. Each year we hosted a large party, and this meant transforming the backyard into an outdoor dining area, much like a Greek taverna. Multicoloured lights were strewn across the yard, outdoor speakers were connected to the His Master's Voice record pick-up, all in readiness for the Greek dancing that would take place.

My mother would spend days preparing traditional Greek sweets to serve on a buffet dessert table. There would be plates piled high with kourambiedes (crescent-shaped, shortbread biscuits sprinkled with icing sugar) and finikia (nut and spice-filled biscuits, baked and dipped in honey syrup and then topped with loose coconut or chopped walnuts).

Finikia were Mum's specialty, and her favourite way of preparing them was to use coconut on top. She also had a special recipe for Ravani tis Mourias, also known as Moriatikos Halvas, an oven-baked semolina cake, cut into diamond shapes, each topped with a blanched almond. This recipe is exclusive to the area surrounding Pyrgos Ilias and isn't found anywhere else in Greece. The piece de resistance however, was Pantespani.; a light sponge cake made with eggs, semolina and flour, that has a sugar syrup poured over it after baking, before being sprinkled with ground cinnamon. This was one of Mum's specialties and is truly a delectable cake. And of course what would a party be without a chocolate cake – but not just any chocolate cake. Mum's was baked high, rich in chocolate and moistened with syrup. It was then cut into diamond shapes (Greeks love diamond shapes!) and sprinkled with desiccated coconut. Exquisite!

The food prepared was plentiful, delicious and traditional; roast lamb rubbed with rigani (Greek oregano), yemista (rice and herb-stuffed tomatoes), yourvalakia (meatballs with rice, cooked in a tomato sauce), chicken wings seasoned with rigani and drizzled with freshly squeezed lemon juice, baked spaghetti in tomato salsa, lots and lots of salads (especially the horiatiki salata that contained copious amounts of Dad's home grown tomatoes and cucumbers) beautifully prepared tarama dip topped with a parsley leaf and kalamata olive for garnish, tzatziki made from cucumbers and strained natural yoghurt, bowls of homemade kalamata olives, plates piled with three types of cheeses (including feta, kefalograviera, kasseri) and much, much more.

As the guests arrived they would always present a gift for my Dad or for the home, and sometimes guests brought lovely boxes of chocolate too! The types of gifts given might include a shirt, a bottle of whiskey or ouzo, a plate of homemade sweets, or an ornament for the home. Guests would never come empty handed; it's tradition to bring gifts and show appreciation for the host family.

As well as the lovely selection of Mum's homemade sweets, the buffet always included juicy wedges of watermelon, bowls of ripe dark cherries, fresh apricots or sultana grapes from our garden, and of course the sweets given to us by the guests.

My parents were very generous hosts and loved to put on a wonderful celebration. We enjoyed having everyone over and watching the grown ups look so lovely, lively and happy. My mother put a great deal of effort into Dad's name day celebrations, as she did with everything in life, and she also presented herself beautifully and elegantly. These were very happy times.

φιλοσοφια

Philosophy

"The basis of a democratic state is liberty."

Aristotle

Two important celebrations held on 25th March
Evangelismos and Greek Independence Day

Evangelismos

The 25th of March marks the celebration of The Annunciation of the Theotokos, also known in Greek as Evangelismos. This is when the Archangel Gabriel appeared to Mary and announced that she would bear the Son of God. It is nine months until Christmas, the birth of Christ.

Usually this feast day falls during the Easter Great Lent. Although one is expected to follow the rules of fasting, it is permissible to eat fish on this day. Those named Evangelia or Evangelos celebrate their name day today.

Greek Independence Day

Greek Independence Day is an annual celebration held on 25th March. It commemorates the beginning of the War of Independence that occurred in 1821, when Bishop Germanos of Patras raised the flag of revolution over the Monastery of Agia Lavra in the Peloponnese. It is a national holiday in Greece and a day that is highly respected and observed by Greeks worldwide.

Revolutionaries cried, "Zito H Ellas!" ("Long Live Greece!") and "Eleftheria H Thanatos!" ("Freedom or Death!") as they began the revolt against the Ottoman Empire, and the 400 years of oppression that had begun in 1453 with the fall of Constantinople.

Greeks fought for their freedom, their heritage and their religion. The War of Independence lasted some eight years until 1829, when parts of Greece finally became independent, however it took many years before all of Greece was liberated. During the years of oppression the church conducted secret schools (krypha scholia) to continue the teachings of Greek language, religion and history.

Just some of the heroes of this revolution are Theodoros Kolokotronis, Laskarina Bouboulina, Nikitaras Papaflessas, George Karaiskakis, and Gregorios Diakos. Amongst the many people who supported the uprising was the English poet, Lord Byron of England, who was known as a philhellene and whom the Greeks consider a national hero.

The church service for commemorating these two important events, Greek Independence Day and The Annunciation of the Theotokos, is both a very moving and patriotic service. The church is decorated with flags and is filled with families and school children who are dressed in national costume or blue and white outfits.

At the end of the service, heartfelt speeches are delivered to honour and remember those who began the uprising, and to respectfully remember those who lost their lives for the liberty of Greece.

School children march in their blue and white school uniforms, holding Greek flags, before assembling at the Shrine of Remembrance together with church leaders, politicians and members of the military. Speeches are delivered to remember and celebrate freedom and independence, unity of the community, the sacrifices made by the heroes of the uprising, and to always remember the difficult and courageous journey of those who took the steps towards liberation. It is a deeply patriotic day, culminating in parades and tributes to ancestors who started and fought for independence. Government officials, church leaders, community leaders and members of the military, lay wreaths to remember the fallen soldiers. This is then followed by a recital of the last stanza of the Ode of Remembrance:

They shall grow not old, as we that are left grow old:
Age shall not weary them, nor the years condemn.
At the going down of the sun and in the morning,
We will remember them.

The Last Post bugle call is respectfully observed – followed by the Greek national anthem and the Australian national anthem.

As was customary for children of my generation, it was necessary for us to attend after hours Greek language school. We did this for some years, attending twice a week. This also meant that we partook in the school celebrations and were dressed in our white shirt, dark blue skirts, white socks and polished black shoes, standing on stage and reciting poems in Greek. I was always very nervous about this but managed to get through, thankfully! My children also attended Greek school and Greek dance classes and took part in these important cultural events.

Secret School
Krifo Sholio

Between the 15th and 19th centuries, when Greece was under Ottoman Rule, Greek history explains that the Krifo Scholio (Secret School) existed to provide basic education and to keep alive the Greek language, literacy and religion. It is thought that these secret schools were held in monasteries and churches. A painting dated 1885/6 by Nikolaos Gyzis titled 'To Krifo Scholio' depicts this part of Greek history.

A nursery rhyme tells that secret schools existed, and that typically the education took place at night.

Greek Verse

Φεγγαράκι μου λαμπρό,
Φέγγε μου να περπατώ,
Να πηγαίνω στο σχολειό
Να μαθαίνω γράμματα,
Γράμματα σπουδάματα
Του Θεού τα πράματα.

English translation

My bright moon
Shine so that I may walk,
To attend school
To learn how to read
And how to write,
And to study God's lessons

Greek Flag

The striking blue and white flag of Greece is easily recognizable, with its white cross in the upper left hand corner signifying the Greek Orthodox religion. It is said that the blue stripes represent the sea and the white stripes represent the waves.

The nine equal horizontal stripes of alternating blue and white are said to represent the number of syllables in the Greek phrase E-lef-ther-i-a i Tha-na-tos meaning 'Freedom or Death', which was the battle cry during the Greek War of Independence.

φιλοσοφια

Philosophy

"We must wait until the evening to see how splendid the day has been."

Sophocles

Masquerade

Apokries is the Greek Carnival tradition, and is celebrated all over Greece during the three week period preceding Kathari Deftera (Clean Monday), the beginning of the Great Lent.

Children and adults follow the tradition of dressing up for Apokries. It is a time of parades, huge feasts, costume and masque parties, and of course lots of kefi. In Greece, Apokries started in Ancient times. It is believed to be a show of worship to Dionysos, the God of Wine and Feast. In more modern times in the Orthodox tradition, Apokries is the preparation period before Lent, and literally means saying goodbye to meat, as this festival precedes the Great Lent of Easter.

As Apokries precedes the commencement of Great Lent for Easter, it allows for gradual abstention of certain foods, beginning with meat, fish and poultry, then dairy foods, and finally oil and wine – but not before the great frivolity of Masquerade is celebrated.

Tanti Auguri a
Tanti

First Week of Apokries

Apokries begins with the opening of the book, Triodion (Orthodox liturgical book). The period of the Triodion can be divided into three sections. The first is the pre-Lenten period, the second is The Forty Days of the Great Fast, and the third is Holy Week. Meat may be eaten during the first week of Apokries.

Second Week of Apokries

The second week of Apokries is the last week of eating meat, and Meatfare Sunday is officially the last day before Easter for eating meat.

Third Week of Apokries

The third week of Apokries is known as Cheese Week. Meat is no longer permitted until after Lent. During this third week, people eat mostly dairy products and eggs. Fish is also allowed. On the Saturday preceding Cheesefare Sunday the Church observes the Saturday of Souls, when memorials are conducted for those who have passed. The final day of Apokries is Cheesefare Sunday and this is the eve of Great Lent.

Usually carnival and masquerade parades are held on this last day of Apokries. It is also the last day that weddings are allowed to take place until after Easter. The Greek Orthodox church follows the tradition that weddings and celebrations cannot take place during the 40 days of Lent. The traditional greeting for this time is, "Kales Apokries", meaning 'Happy Carnival'.

Clean Monday

Clean Monday marks the end of Apokries and Carnival and is the first day of the 40 day Lenten Fast also known as Sarakosti. This is the spiritual fasting in preparation for Easter and traditionally no meat, fish, eggs, dairy products or oil are allowed to be eaten for the 40 days leading up to Easter. Exceptions include Palm Sunday and the 25th of March (the Annunciation), when it is permitted to eat fish. In Greece, Clean Monday is a National Public Holiday, and families and friends take excursions to the mountains or the beach to enjoy a Lenten picnic meal, and perhaps fly a kite.

Foods allowed during the fasting periods are called Nistisima (fasting) and these include pulses, beans, calamari, octopus, shellfish, taramaslata (caviar dip), and an asortment of pickles. For sweets, it is traditional to have the delicately delicious Lenten cake with its aroma of orange and bursts of sweetness from the currants, or the grainy-textured, cinnamon and honey infused Halva that has been made with sunflower oil, or the ready made Halva made with tahini.

φιλοσοφια

Philosophy

"Well begun is half done."

Aristotle

Lagana Bread

Clean Monday Bread

Lagana is a traditional flat bread prepared especially for Clean Monday, the start of the 40-day Greek Orthodox Easter Lenten Fast. This unleavened bread has quite a distinctive look as the top has finger print indents across the surface, and it is adorned with a sprinkling of sesame seeds prior to baking. Tradition dictates that the bread is pulled apart for serving rather than using a knife to cut into slices.

Ingredients

3 1/2 cups finely milled plain flour

1 tablespoon yeast

1 1/2 tablespoons sugar

1 1/3 cups warm water

1 teaspoon salt

2 tablespoon sunflower oil

1/2 cup sesame seeds for sprinkling

Method

Preheat oven to a low.

Combine yeast, 1 teaspoon of sugar and 1/4 of a cup of the warm water.

Cover with a clean cloth, place into the warm oven to activate.

In a large bowl combine the flour, salt, and the remainderof the sugar.

Make a well in the centre and pour in the sunflour oil, the warm water and add the activated yeast mixture.

Mix well and then turn the dough out onto a floured surface and knead for approximately 10 minutes until smooth.

Place the ball of dough in a large bowl that has been lightly greased with sunflower oil, and cover with clean tea towel and place in the warm oven to rise and double in size. This should take approximately on hour or more.

Punch the dough down and continue kneading for a few minutes.

Using a rolling pin roll the dough out into a rectangle shape and place on a lightly greased backing tray.

Lightly brush with extra sunflower oil and sprinkle with sesame seeds.

Return to the warm oven to rise once again.

Remove from oven, working quickly use your index finger to gently poke holes across the surface of the bread.

Return bread dough to oven, increase the temperature to 180 degrees and bake until golden brown. This should take 15-20 minutes.

During the year other fasting periods are observed, providing an opportunity for spiritual growth and cleansing. The local parish can provide more information about fasting rules, especially for pregnancy, lactation, the aged, and for those with health issues.

Many traditional Greek recipes can be converted to fasting meals and are equally delicious without meat and poultry. It makes for creative cooking and the use of a wonderful assortment of fresh, seasonal vegetables.

On a more delicate matter, it is prescribed that abstinence be observed during the periods of fasting. It is understood that this may be difficult to follow, however it is still recommended to at least abstain prior to receiving Holy Communion.

Weekly Fast

Traditionally the church teaches that fasting occurs on a weekly basis on every Wednesday (betrayal by Judas) and Friday (the commemoration of the suffering of Christ on the Cross). During this time diets are modified to exclude meat, fish with backbones, dairy products, eggs, olive oil, and wine and alcohol. It is permissible to eat shellfish and calamari as these do not contain bones.

Easter Fast
(movable date)

The Great Lenten Fast officially begins on Clean Monday and is observed for 40 days, and then continues throughout the following week known as Holy Week. This spiritual period is a time for reflection, prayer, and personal improvement.

During Holy Week, usually the Thursday evening meal is the last full meal taken until Easter. Wine and oil are permitted at this meal.

Good Friday is the strictest fasting day of the Orthodox calendar, and it is customary to not partake of food on this day. Even those who have not observed the Forty Day Lenten Fast usually respectfully observe this day of fasting. After the Easter Saturday morning church service, when communion is taken, it is permissible to have a little wine, fruit juice and fruit as part of a very simple meal. This provides a little sustenance before breaking the fast completely after the Saturday night Resurrection Service.

Fish is permitted on Palm Sunday and on the 25th of March, the Annunciation. It is permissible to prepare fish on these days. Traditionally homemakers prepare Bakaliaros (fried cod fish), which is served with Skordalia (garlic sauce), boiled greens or beetroot.

Dormition of the Theotokos Fast

August 1st to 14th

The fast for the Dormition ('falling asleep') of the Theotokos (Mary, Mother of God) takes place from 1 – 14 August. This two week fast is similar to the fast of Great Lent.

From Monday through to Friday a strict fast is observed, however wine and oil are permitted on Saturdays and Sundays, and fish may be eaten on the 6th of August for the Transfiguration of Christ.

The feast day for the falling asleep of Mary takes place on the 15th of August.

Nativity Fast

November 15th to December 24th

Strict fasting is observed on each Monday, Wednesday and Friday during this period. On each Tuesday, Thursday, Saturday and Sunday, oil, wine and fish are permitted, until 13th of December when fish is no longer allowed. The Feast Day is on Christmas Day.

Individual Fasting Days

January 5th (Eve of Epiphany), August 29th (Beheading of St. John the Baptist) and September 14th (the feast of the Elevation of the Holy Cross) are important fasting dates in the Greek Orthodox Calendar, and a strict fast is observed on these days. Wine and oil are permitted.

Greek cuisine includes a vast variety of
seasonal vegetables and seafood.
Meat is usually limited and this makes it easy to
convert traditional recipes into fasting meals that are
equally delicious without the addition of meat and
poultry. Modify your favourite recipes and you'll be
surprised at just how delicious they can be.
I've included some of my favourite
Lenten foods.

Lentil Soup

Simple to make, Fakes is a a nutritious, healthy and hearty soup with an exquisite taste. An alternative option is to add tomato paste, diced carrots and finely chopped celery. Prepared either way, you will love this delicious soup served with crusty continental bread.

Ingredients

2 cups small brown lentils

1 onion, finely chopped

1 clove garlic, roughly chopped

1/2 cup olive oil

1/4 teaspoon oregano

3 bay leaves

8 cups water

Salt and pepper

White vinegar, to serve

Method

Place lentils on a table, check and remove any grit.

Wash the lentils and drain.

Add olive oil to a heavy-based saucepan and gently fry onion until soft.

Add lentils and cook for 2 minutes.

Add all other ingredients and bring to the boil.

Reduce heat and simmer for 1-2 hours, or until lentils and vegetables are soft.

Serve with a dash of white vinegar, and crusty bread.

Fáva

Split Pea Soup

Fava is a delicious, hearty and nutritious soup that is quick and easy to make. This recipe makes a thick and creamy version, but if preferred add some extra water during cooking to make a thinner soup. Serve with a drizzle of extra virgin olive oil, a splash of freshly squeezed lemon juice, ground black pepper, and crusty bread.

Ingredients

2 cups yellow split peas

6 cups water

1 onion, finely chopped

1-2 teaspoons of sea salt, or to taste

1/4 teaspoon of white pepper

4 tablespoons olive oil

To serve

extra virgin olive oil

lemon wedges

Method

Boil 4 cups of water in the kettle.

Place lentils on a table, check over and remove any grit or discoloured peas.

In a heavy-based saucepan, heat the olive oil, and gently fry the onion.

Add the yellow split peas and stir for 1-2 minutes.

Pour over the boiled water and simmer gently for 45 minutes or until soft.

Stir in the salt and pepper.

Serve Fava into bowls.

Place the olive oil and lemon wedges onto the dining table, ready to add as seasoning for this thick hearty soup.

Serve with crusty bread.

Chickpea Soup

Revithia Soup needs a little time to plan ahead as the chickpeas require soaking overnight. It is however a hearty , healthy and highly nutritious soup that is simple to prepare. Enjoy with crusty continental bread.

Ingredients

500 grams chickpeas, soaked overnight and drained

1 onion, finely chopped

2 carrots, chopped

2 celery sticks, chopped

2 cups chopped spinach

1 can of whole tomatoes, pureed

7 cups of water

1/2 cup of olive oil

Salt and pepper

Method

In a heavy-based pot, heat the oil and fry the onion, carrots and celery for a few minutes or until the onion is soft.

Add all other ingredients and simmer gently for 2 hours or until the chickpeas are tender.

Season to taste.

Serve with fresh crusty bread.

Fasolátha

White Bean Soup

Fassolatha is a staple of Greece that is enjoyed as a hearty main meal all year round. The addition of tomato is optional, but essential to enjoying this highly nutritious and hearty soup is an extra drizzle of virgin olive oil when serving. Quite Simply, it's food for the soul!

Ingredients

2 cups dried cannellini, haricot or lima beans

7 cups of water, boiled

1 onion, finely chopped

1 small clove of garlic, finely chopped

2 carrots, chopped

2 celery sticks with leaves, chopped

3/4 cup olive oil

1 can of whole tomatoes, pureed

1-2 tablespoons of tomato paste

1/4 teaspoon ground black pepper

1/2 teaspoon sugar

1 teaspoon salt

2 tablespoons of finely chopped parsley

Method

Wash the beans and soak for 2 hours, then drain.

In a large pot, heat the oil and fry the onion for 5 minutes. Add the carrots and celery and continue frying for 2 minutes, add the garlic and fry for 1 minute.

Add all other ingredients and bring to the boil. Simmer for 2 hours, or until tender.

Season to taste.

Sprinkle with additional chopped parsley, and serve with fresh crusty bread.

Spanakórizo

Spinach Rice

Spanakorizo is a spinach and rice dish that can either be made with fresh lemon juice or chopped fresh tomato, and can be enjoyed either hot or cold, as a main or as an accompaniment. This Greek spinach rice recipe is nutritious and delicious and the use of baby spinach that is still on the stems together with the addition of fresh herbs and a generous amount of olive oil enlivens this simple yet delicious vegetarian dish.

Ingredients

1 kg spinach

1/2 cup olive oil

1 cup medium grain rice

1 cup spring onion, chopped

1/4 cup fresh dill, cut finely

1/4 cup fresh parsley, cut finely

2 cups hot water from the kettle

Lemon wedges

Method

Wash and rinse the spinach well, and roughly chop.

Heat the oil in a heavy-based saucepan and sauté the spring onion and rice.

Cook for 2-3 minutes.

Add the chopped spinach and stir.

Add the 2 cups of boiling water and herbs.

Season with salt and pepper and continue to cook.

When ready, remove from the heat and serve immediately with a wedge of lemon.

Alternatively, for a tomato-based recipe add some tomato salsa or paste with the hot water, and omit the lemon.

Spanakorizo can be enjoyed cold the next day.

Fried Calamari

Fried calamari is a wonderfully delicious meze served with fresh lemon wedges and enjoyed with a glass of ouzo, or as a main meal accompanied by a green salad. My mother would place her flour mixture onto a couple of sheets of newspapers and then toss the calamari through whilst also lifting the sides of the newspaper to help coat the tentacles and rings of the squid in the floury mixture. Working quickly she would take a few at a time and place them into hot oil to fry for just a few minutes to ensure that they stay tender and light golden brown in colour.

Ingredients

1 kg squid, younger is best

Sunflower oil for frying

Lemon wedges for serving

Flour mixture

1 teaspoon sea salt

1/4 teaspoon ground black pepper

1/2 teaspoon oregano, rubbed between your hands

1/2 cup plain flour, sifted

1/4 cup cornflour, sifted

Method

Carefully clean the squid, and cut into halves lengthways. Cut into 5mm strips.

Heat the oil in a pan until hot.

Take a large piece of baking paper and place the flour mixture ingredients on top. Mix through using the tines of a fork.

Dip the calamari into the flour mixture, shake off the excess and place into the frying pan a few at a time. Turn down the heat and cook for 1-2 minutes.

Drain well on absorbent kitchen paper and place on a serving dish with lemon wedges.

Tomato Salsa
with Rigani

Ingredients

6 whole tomatoes, peeled and chopped

1/4 cup olive oil

Salt and pepper

1/4 teaspoon oregano, rubbed between the hands

Method

Place all ingredients into a heavy-based saucepan and bring to the boil.

Reduce the heat and simmer until thick.

Serve with your favourite pasta.

Ingredients

6 whole tomatoes, peeled and chopped

¼ cup olive oil

Salt and pepper

1 quill of cinnamon

¼ of a glass of red wine

Method

Place all ingredients into a heavy-based saucepan and bring to the boil.

Reduce the heat and simmer until thick.

Serve with your favourite pasta, or over grilled eggplant.

Prawn Saganaki

Prawns baked in Tomato Sauce

Prawn Saganaki is a delicious way to enjoy Greek style seafood. A rich and thick tomato sauce is prepared before fresh uncooked prawns are added to the pan or baking dish, and cooked for just a few minutes before being sprinkled with feta cheese. This dish makes a lovely meze to be enjoyed with ouzo, or as a main meal served with pilafi rice or bread, a leafy green salad and a glass of chilled retsina.

Ingredients

500 grams of green prawns, peeled and deveined

2 spring onions, chopped

1 clove garlic, crushed

1/2 cup olive oil

2 cups tomatoes, peeled and chopped

1/2 cup dry white wine

1 tablespoon parsley, finely chopped

1/2 teaspoon oregano, rubbed between the hands

1/2 teaspoon sugar

1/4 teaspoon pepper

1 teaspoon salt

Method

In a pot add the oil and heat gently.

Add the spring onions and fry for 2-3 minutes.

Add garlic and fry for 1 minute

Add all the other ingredients and cook until the sauce is reduced, thick and rich.

Transfer the sauce into a baking dish, add the prawns and bake in a hot oven for 15 minutes.

Serve immediately with crusty bread.

** For a non-fasting version, top the sauce with crumbed feta before placing the dish into the hot oven.

Briami

Baked Vegetables

Briami is a traditional recipe for baked seasonal vegetables. This delicious meal is easy to make and is especially flavoursome when made in summer when there is an abundance of eggplant, zucchinis, and tomatoes. The vegetables are placed into a baking dish together with sliced onions, fresh herbs and then drizzled with a generous amount of olive oil. Briami can be enjoyed as a main meal served with fresh bread or alternatively as a side dish.

Ingredients

1 onion, peeled and sliced

2 zucchini, sliced

1 red capsicum, sliced

1 eggplant, cut into eight

5 potatoes, cut into six wedges

2 cups tomatoes, peeled and chopped

2 tablespoons chopped parsley

1/2 cup olive oil

1/2 teaspoon sugar

1 teaspoon salt

1/4 teaspoon ground black pepper

Method

Wash the eggplant and cut into eight pieces.

Place into a colander and sprinkle with salt. This helps reduce any bitterness.

Prepare all other ingredients and place into a baking dish.

Mix well to cover with herbs and olive oil and bake for 1-1/2 hours in a moderate oven until all ingredients are cooked through.

Briami can be served either hot or cold and is best served with some lovely rustic bread to mop up the plate with.

Green Bean and Potato Stew

Fassolakia me Patates is a classic Greek vegetarian recipe made with stringless green beans and potatoes. It's an easy, delicious and rustic meal, and so very nutritious too!

Ingredients

500 grams stringless beans, topped and tailed

1 large onion, finely chopped

1 clove garlic, crushed

3 large potatoes, cut into 6 wedges

1 tin whole tomatoes, pureed

1/2 cup olive oil

1 1/2 cups water

Salt and pepper

2 tablespoons chopped parsley

Method

In a large pot, heat the olive oil and sauté the onion until soft.

Add the beans, and sauté for a few minutes.

Add the garlic and stir for 1 minute.

Add the tomatoes, salt, pepper, parsley and water.

Add the potatoes and continue cooking until the vegetables are tender.

Serve with fresh crusty bread.

Aginares me Arakas

Artichokes with Peas

Artichoke hearts and baby peas make a delicious and simple vegetarian meal. Generous amounts of lemon juice and olive oil and a good sprinkling of fresh dill make a wonderful dish to be enjoyed as a main meal served with fresh bread.

Ingredients

12 medium artichokes, fresh or frozen

2 medium onions, sliced

4 medium potatoes, peeled and cut into half and then into thirds

3 carrots, peeled and cut into 2 inch rounds

1/4 cup olive oil

1 tablespoon tomato paste

2 cups hot water from the kettle

1/3 cup chopped fresh dill

1 cup frozen peas (thawed)

salt and pepper

Method

If using fresh artichokes trim and clean them.

In a heavy based saucepan, heat the oil and add onions and cook until transparent.

Add the potatoes and carrots and cook over medium heat for 15-20 minutes.

Add the tomato paste, artichokes and enough hot water to cover.

Bring to the boil, season, cover and reduce heat.

Cook for another 10 minutes or until artichokes are tender and potatoes and carrots are cooked

Add the dill and peas and stir gently.

Cook for 3-5 minutes and then remove from heat.

Serve hot with a wedge of lemon to squeeze on top, and some crusty bread.

Bakaliáros Tiganitós

Fried Salted Cod

Bakalarios is a traditional fried salted cod recipe that is perfectly accompanied by skordalia (garlic sauce), bantzaria (boiled beetroot salad) and horta (wild greens).

Ingredients

500 grams dried salted cod

Sunflower oil for frying

Lemon wedges for serving

Batter

1/2 cup plain flour

1/4 cup corn flour

1/4 teaspoon pepper

1 teaspoon salt

1/3 cup warm water

Method

Remove the skin from the cod, and cut into 3-inch pieces. Rinse off the salt.

In a clean glass bowl, soak the cod pieces in water for approximately 12 hours in the refrigerator, making sure to change the water several times.

Drain and remove any visible bones, and then allow the cod to drain well.

Prepare the batter and heat the oil in a large frypan.

Dip the cod pieces into the batter and fry in the hot oil. Lower the heat to medium and fry until golden brown on both sides.

Drain on absorbent kitchen paper.

Serve with garlic sauce, boiled greens, and a beetroot salad.

My mother spent an entire morning making her traditional Skordalia, which was also one of her specialties. Whole washed potatoes are boiled until soft. A delicate fish stock is made from simmering a couple of small fish heads in a separate pot. In the mortar and pestle that Mum purchased in Zakynthos as a young bride and later brought with her all the way to Australia, she would place a few whole garlic cloves and a good teaspoon of salt and begin working the garlic and salt into a mash. The hot cooked potatoes would be carefully hand peeled and added to the mortar and worked with the garlic together with a generous amount of virgin olive oil and a splash of white vinegar. The fish stock would be added gradually until the skordalia became smooth and elastic in consistency. The seasoning would be checked and adjusted to taste. Making Skordialia in a mortar and pestle took much expert skill to get it just right, but the effort was well worth it!

The recipe provided here is a fasting recipe especially for Lent.

Ingredients

1/2 to 4 cloves of garlic (depending on taste)

1/2 teaspoon salt

3 tablespoons of white vinegar

1 cup of stale bread pieces, chopped

1/4 cup of water

1/4 cup of olive oil

Method

Remove crusts from bread and cut roughly into pieces.

Place into an electric blender and add the garlic, salt, olive oil and vinegar.

Blend and gradually add water until the consistency is smooth.

Make necessary adjustment to the taste to prepare the sauce to your liking.

This is a delicious and healthy salad made from boiled beets and dressed simply with extra virgin olive oil and vinegar. In Greece, and especially from my father's birthplace, beetroot is also called kokinogoulia.

Ingredients

1 bunch of beetroot

Extra virgin olive oil

Vinegar – red or white

Method

Take the whole bunch of beetroot and cut off the greens. Wash and rinse several times to ensure that no dirt remains. Separate the red stems from the leaves and put them both aside in separate bowls.

Scrub the beets well, and cook in boiling salted water for approximately 20 minutes, then add the stems. Cook for a further 5 minutes, and then add the leaves and cook until the beets are tender.

Skin the beets, chop into bite-sized pieces and place into a bowl. Top with boiled leaves and stems.

Dress to taste with extra virgin olive oil, vinegar and salt.

Boiled Greens

Horta is a general term used to described seasonal leafy greens. These greens are then washed, boiled and dressed in olive oil, lemon juice or vinegar and sprinkled with salt, before serving. Horta are a wonderful and nutritious accompaniment to many dishes; especially seafood and grilled meats. To dress the Horta, vinegar is used more often than not for Vlita, and lemon juice is usually used to dress the other types of leafy greens.

Ingredients

Leafy Greens (Amaranthus, Dandelions or Endive)

Extra Virgin Olive Oil

Lemon Juice or Vinegar

Salt

Method

Place a large pot half filled with water on the stove and bring to the boil.

Take the carefully washed leafy greens, that have had discoloured leaves, thick stalks and roots removed, and roughly chop into thirds.

Add a teaspoon of salt to the pot and then carefully add the washed leafy greens.

Stir and then bring to the boil before reducing the heat slightly to a slow boil.

Cook the greens for approximately 20 minutes, until tender.

If using dandelions, these usually take longer to cook as the leaves are just that little bit tougher.

When ready, empty the pot into a colander and drain well, or reserve some of the cooking water for a nutritious drink to be enjoyed with fresh lemon juice added.

Place the horta into a shallow open serving bowl and dress with a generous amount of extra virgin olive oil, either lemon juice or vinegar, and salt.

Mix well.

To Serve

When serving place a bottle of extra virgin olive oil on the table together with a plate of lemon wedges and small bottle of vinegar so that guests can add more dressing to suit their personal liking.

Taramá

Fish Roe Dip

Tarama is a creamy fish roe dip made with stale bread, a generous amount of olive oil and the juice of fresh lemons to give it that lovely tangy taste. It's best served with warm pita bread that has been sprinkled with a little sea salt, or fresh rustic, crusty bread.

Ingredients

1 heaped tablespoon of Tarama fish roe

4 pieces of stale white bread

1/3 cup water

1/2 cup olive oil

1/3 cup lemon juice

1/4 teaspoon grated onion (optional or to taste)

Method

Place all ingredients into a blender and process until smooth.

Make the necessary adjustments to taste to prepare the sauce to your liking, either adding a little more oil or lemon juice to get the consistency just right.

Place into a serving bowl and decorate with a sprig of parsley or dill and a pitted kalamata olive.

Lenten Cake

Lenten cake is a dense cake made with raisins, currents and chopped walnuts and infused with aromatic spices and orange. This is an egg and dairy free cake that is a delicious treat to be enjoyed during Lent, or at any other time!

Ingredients

3 cups plain flour

2 teaspoons baking powder

1 teaspoon cinnamon

cup each of currants, sultanas and chopped walnuts

2/3 cup sunflower oil

1 cup sugar

1 cup orange juice

1 tablespoon grated orange rind

Icing sugar

Method

Sift together the flour, baking powder and cinnamon.

Add the fruits.

Beat together the oil, sugar, orange juice and orange rind.

Add the dry ingredients and stir until combined thoroughly.

Pour the mixture into a 13x9 inch baking pan and bake for 45 minutes in a moderate oven.

When cool, sprinkle with the sifted icing sugar.

Moustokouloura

Grape Must Biscuits

Moustokouloura are delicious and aromatic biscuits made with grape must (petimezi) from boiled and reduced fresh grape juice especially put aside during the wine-making process. The grape must and cinnamon makes these biscuits a richer and deeper colour, and the texture and taste make them a perfect accompaniment to a cup of Greek coffee. When petemizi has been unavailable, I have successfully made moustokouloura using red table wine.

Ingredients

4 cups plain flour

3/4 cup caster sugar

2 teaspoons baking power

1 teaspoon cinnamon

3/4 cup sunflower oil

3/4 cup petimezi

1/2 cup orange juice

Method

Sift the dry ingredients.

Combine the sugar, petimezi, orange juice and sunflower oil and pour into the dry ingredients.

Form into a dough, knead and transfer to a lightly floured surface.

Continue to knead, adding more flour as required.

Take walnut-sized pieces of the dough, roll out into pencil-sized lengths and form loose circles with overlapped edges.

Place onto lightly greased baking trays and bake for 30-40 minutes.

Halva

Semolina Cake

Halva is a delicious semolina cake that is initially toasted and then infused with cinnamon, and moistened with a honey and sugar syrup. The result is an aromatic, grainy textured cake that is simply divine!

Ingredients

1/4 cup sunflower oil

1 cup course ground semolina

2 teaspoons ground cinnamon

Syrup

3/4 cup sugar

1/4 cup honey

2 cups of water

1 cinnamon quill

Method

Place all the syrup ingredients into a pot and stir until the sugar is dissolved. Gently bring to the boil, reduce the heat and simmer for 5 minutes.

Whilst the syrup is simmering, place the sunflower oil and semolina in a heavy-based pot.

Keep stirring to gently toast the semolina until it is a deep golden colour, and add the ground cinnamon. Stir.

Remove both pots from the stove.

Gradually add the hot syrup into the toasted semolina mixture. (Be careful as the semolina will start to bubble and may splatter.)

When all the syrup has been added, take the pot back to the stove and stir until the mixture comes away from the side of the pot.

Cover with a clean tea towel and place the lid on top. Stand for 15 minutes.

Place the mixture into a mould or baking dish and spread evenly.

Sprinkle with a little extra cinnamon and cool.

Πάσχα

The celebration of Easter is a movable date and is calculated as the first Sunday after the full moon on or after the vernal equinox. This calculation is identical for both Western and Orthodox Easters but the churches base the dates on different calendars; Western churches use the Gregorian calendar and the Orthodox churches use the older Julian calendar.

Much spiritual preparation is observed during this time, especially when adhering to the protocols for Apokries and the forty days of Great Lent. Families follow the rituals of fasting and spiritual growth, as well as preparing for the celebration of Easter; new outfits are purchased and in Greece, homes are whitewashed and spring-cleaned in preparation for the family to gather for the festivities.

Easter Holy Week

During Holy Week the Greek Orthodox Church holds church services each day, and on some days there are morning, afternoon and evening services.

Palm Sunday

Morning: Matins and Divine Liturgy
Evening: The Matins of Holy Monday

Holy Monday

Evening: The Matins of Holy Tuesday

Holy Tuesday

Evening: The Matins of Holy Wednesday

Holy Wednesday

Morning: Pre-Sanctified Divine Liturgy
Evening: Matins of Holy Thursday-Holy Unction (Efchelaion)

Holy Thursday

Morning: Vespers and Divine Liturgy of St. Basil the Great followed by Communion
Evening: Holy Passion of our Lord Jesus Christ and The reading of The Twelve Gospels

Good Friday

Morning: Service of Imperial Hours and dressing of the Epitaph
Afternoon: Good Friday Vespers (Apokathilosis)
Evening: The Matins of Holy Saturday. Service of the Epitaph

Easter Saturday

Morning: Vespers and Divine Liturgy of St. Basil the Great
followed by Holy Communion
Evening: 11pm service of the Midnight Office
12 midnight The Holy Resurrection Service and the
Divine Liturgy of St. John Chrysostom until 2.30am.

Good Friday

Megali Paraskevi

Good Friday is considered a day of mourning and therefore it is customary not to cook, bake, sew or work. All Easter baking is either done on Holy Thursday or Easter Saturday.

On Friday morning the Service of Imperial Hours takes place, as does the dressing of the Kavouklion, the ornately carved wooden stand used for the Easter service. The Kavouklion is adorned with an icon and many hundreds of flowers, and parish volunteers gather at the church to offer their assistance. The perfume of these many flowers, and that of basil, fills the church with the most beautiful scent.

The Epitaphio is a cloth depicting Christ being removed from the Cross; it represents the body of Christ. The afternoon Good Friday Vespers known as the Apokathilosis is a very moving service where symbolically the body of Christ is taken down from the cross and is placed onto the adorned Kavouklion.

At the evening Good Friday service the Epitaphios (Kavouklion adorned with flowers and cloth depicting Christ) is carried out of the church by the male parish helpers. The priest then leads a slow procession around the neighbourhood, and followers carry lit candles throughout this reverent and solemn service. The Epitaphio is returned to the church entrance for the procession to walk beneath, and when everyone has re-entered the church the Epitaphio is placed at the altar. At the end of the service the priest hands out cuttings of basil and flowers for parishioners to take home with them. The traditional greeting before the resurrection service is, “Kalo Pascha” (“Happy Easter”) or “Kali Anastasi” (“Happy Resurrection”).

Easter Saturday
Resurrection Service

Easter is about renewal and rebirth. In Greece Easter falls in the spring, perfectly demonstrating these themes of renewal and rebirth. Just before midnight the lights in the church are switched off, the candles are extinguished and the church falls into complete darkness whilst the resurrection prayers are read. At the stroke of midnight, the priest emerges with a lit candle and proceeds to light the candles of the eager congregation members who wait to receive the first light. They in turn pass the light on, and one by one the candles illuminate the church in a magnificent glow to represent the New Light. Congregation members respectfully and quietly kiss and greet one another with good wishes for “Kali Anastasi” (“Happy Resurrection”).

The priest then leads the congregation quietly outside and the congregation assembles at the front of the church, spilling out onto the streets with their lit candles. The church bells toll, and the priest and psalmists together with the congregation chant, “Christos Anesti Eknekron” (“Christ has risen from the dead”) three times.

The traditional greeting after the resurrection service is, “Christos Anesti” (“Christ has risen”). Communion may be taken at the end of this service, which usually concludes around 3am.

There is a special sequence that is followed when greeting one another for Easter. One greets with, “Christos Anesti” (“Christ has Risen”), the other replies, “Alithos Anesti” (“Truly Risen”).

It is traditional to take home the lit candle and the new light that it represents. Some parishes sell already prepared candles in a decorated cup, and these may be purchased prior to the service. Lanterns may be brought from home or a candle that has been placed through a foil-wrapped disposable cup can do an equally good job. The most important thing is to protect the flame from the wind so that it may be brought into the home to bring the blessing of the new light.

Many families, especially those with elderly parents or young children, will leave the church after the midnight resurrection service and partake of a small midnight feast to break the fast of Great Lent, and to celebrate the resurrection of Christ.

Prior to entering their homes many people will use the lit candle to mark a cross on the doorway entrance of their home, before proceeding to light the candles in the candelabras that are sitting on the dining table, set ready for the breaking of the fast supper. Kandilia (oil lamps) used for memorials may also be lit.

Resurrection Feast

At the end of the Saturday evening Resurrection Service families gather to enjoy a small feast to break the Forty Day Lenten Fast.

In our family, we serve Avgolemeno (Chicken Soup) followed by tiny portions of quail, braised liver, lemon and oregano chicken, baked lemon and oregano potatoes, Tsoureki (Easter bread), Koulourakia (Easter biscuits) and red-dyed eggs. Other families may serve the traditional Mayeritsa (lamb's entrails soup) instead of Avgolemono soup.

The supper takes place at around 1AM, so the portions are very small. The table setting is traditional with plates of red-dyed eggs and koulourakia adorning the table. Before taking part in the supper, the family first sings "Hristos Anesti", followed by cheers to our good health, stin iyeia mas!

Those named Anastasi, Anastasia, Lambros and Lambrini celebrate their name day after the Holy Saturday resurrection service. It is usual to extend wishes of "Hronia Polla" ("Many Years") at the service.

Hristos Anesti Hymn

Greek Verse	English translation
Χριστός ανέστη εκ νεκρών,	*Christ is risen from the dead,*
θανάτω θάνατον πατήσας,	*Trampling down death by death,*
και τοις εν τοις μνήμασι,	*And to those in the tombs*
ζωὴν χαρισάμενος!	*He has given life!*

The Christos Anesti hymn is chanted at Easter to celebrate the moment of Christ's resurrection. It is a truly beautiful and moving hymn, filled with deep emotion. The priest and psalmists alternately repeat the hymn three times, and during the forty days following Easter the hymn is sung at Sunday church services, baptisms, weddings and funerals.

Easter Sunday
Luncheon Feast

The Easter celebration lunch is a family feast. It is traditional for the men of the family to gather early in the morning to prepare the spit-roasted lamb. Family and friends arrive to the inviting aromas of lamb, oregano and lemon that are already permeating the neighbourhood, as the lamb rotates over the charcoal. Alternatively the lamb can be prepared in the oven and roasted slowly until it falls off the bone.

The Luncheon Feast usually consists of an assortment of dips, home-made bread and fresh salads. It is best served with chilled Retsina, the traditional resin-flavoured dry white wine or homemade wine to perfectly compliment the wonderful Greek flavours.

Following lunch the red-dyed eggs are brought to the table for cracking. It is believed that the last person holding an unbroken egg is blessed with good fortune. Afterwards, koulourakia are served with Greek coffee. Frivolity and kefi go hand in hand. And of course music and dancing are an important part of the day.

Greek Butter Biscuits

Koulourakia are prepared for the Easter celebrations and baking occurs during Holy Week, but not on Good Friday. The dough is formed into a variety of shapes, including plaits, twists, coils, braids, figure eights and loose circles with overlapping ends. The delightful aromas of orange and vanilla permeate throughout the home.

Ingredients

1/2 block of unsalted butter, at room temperature (125 grams)

1 cup caster sugar

31/2 cups plain flour

Pinch of salt

1 teaspoon baking powder

3 eggs

1 teaspoon pure vanilla essence

1/3 cup milk or orange juice

Grated orange rind (optional)

Egg glaze

2 egg yolks

2 tablespoons milk

Method

Preheat oven to 190 degrees.

Warm the butter and add to the sifted ingredients.

Knead until the mixture resembles breadcrumbs.

Add the beaten egg, vanilla and continue kneading.

Add milk and extra flour if required, and knead until smooth.

Break off pieces the size of small walnuts and roll out using your hands. Create traditional patterns of twists and coils.

Place the egg glaze ingredients into a small bowl and whisk together with a fork. Using a small pastry brush, glaze the koulourakia before baking.

Bake in a moderate oven for 15-20 minutes. Cool on wire rack.

Greek Verse

"platho, platho koulourakia
me to dio mou to herakia.
O fournos that to pseesse
To speetee tha meereesee."

English translation

"I'm kneading my little biscuits
using my two little hands.
The oven will bake them
The house will be filled with the aroma."

To ensure absolute freshness, it is best to prepare the dyed eggs on Easter Saturday morning and to use white-shelled eggs to enhance the colour.

As is usual in the Orthodox faith, there is much symbolism surrounding red-dyed eggs. The red colour used to dye the eggs represents the blood of Christ and the egg itself symbolizes the renewal of life. Eggs may be dyed other colours, but traditionally Easter is celebrated with red-dyed eggs.

The dyed eggs are cracked at the Easter Saturday midnight supper or at Easter Sunday lunch. Usually the host family prepares the eggs and enough are prepared for each guest to receive their own egg.

The frivolity surrounding the cracking of eggs is much anticipated. Holding the egg firmly, family and friends try to crack each other's egg by gently hitting the end points together, head-on and not at an angle. The winner is the one with an egg that is not completely cracked!

History tells that the egg represents the tomb of Christ, and that the broken eggs are victorious as they represent Christ's resurrection. Through times of need this tradition evolved into what we know today, where the victor (holding an uncracked egg) is allowed to gather the cracked eggs of all their opponents.

Ingredients

12 white-shelled eggs, as fresh as possible

1 packet red dye, available from Greek wholesalers

1 cup white vinegar

A little olive oil, for polishing the eggs

Method

In a stainless steel pot, add the fresh eggs. Add enough cold water to completely cover the eggs.

Dissolve the red dye powder in 1 cup of boiling water and add to the pot. Add the vinegar and gently bring to the boil. Reduce the heat to simmering point, and cook the eggs for around 15-20 minutes.

Remove the eggs using a slotted spoon, rinse gently under warm water and place on a platter lined with absorbent kitchen paper.

When cool, polish the eggs using a piece of kitchen paper that has been slightly dipped into olive oil.

Decorated Red Dyed Eggs

Kokkina Avga

Ingredients

12 white-shelled eggs, as fresh as possible

1 packet red dye, available from Greek wholesalers

1 cup white vinegar

Clean stockings, cut into a length to hold individual eggs

Edible leaves (geranium, dill or parsley) for decorating

A little olive oil, for polishing the eggs

Method

In a stainless steel pot, add the fresh eggs. Add enough cold water to completely cover the eggs, and gently bring to the boil. Reduce the heat to simmering point, and cook the eggs for around 15-20 minutes.

Remove the eggs using a slotted spoon, rinse gently under warm water and place on a platter lined with absorbent kitchen paper.

Decorating the Eggs

Take one cooled egg at a time, and place either a parsley sprig, dill sprig or geranium leaf on one side of the egg.

Take a 3-inch piece of clean nylon stocking, and tie one end.

Stretch the nylon over the egg and tie a knot to close the stocking over the entire egg. It may be useful to have 2 people working on this task.

Preparing Dye

Dissolve the dye in 1 cup of hot water and add ½ cup white vinegar.

In a separate bowl, place enough fresh cold water to cover the eggs. Pour in the cup of dye mixture.

Place the eggs gently into the bowl and allow to sit for approximately 5 minutes.

Return the eggs to their carton and allow them to dry completely before gently cutting the nylon off and revealing the beautiful leaf patterns.

Place the eggs one by one onto a plate covered in paper towels.

Take another paper towel, slightly moisten it with a little olive oil and rub the eggs gently to give them a beautiful, shiny appearance.

Arrange the decorated eggs onto a serving plate or bowl.

Tsoureki, also known as Lambropsomo, literally translates to 'Easter Bread'. This is a delightfully sweet, buttery and aromatic bread. Enjoyed as fresh as possible, it is baked on Easter Saturday morning ready for serving at the midnight supper following the Saturday night resurrection service. This beautifully delicious bread is plaited, and then formed into a loaf or round shape. It is optional to place red-dyed eggs in the centre of the bread before baking. The wonderful aromas of Mahlepi (ground wild cherry) and Masticha (aromatic gum) permeate through the home and fill the senses with anticipation of mouth-watering enjoyment.

Tsoureki

Greek Easter Bread

Ingredients

1 kg plain special plain flour (finely milled flour)

3/4 teaspoon salt

1 teaspoon ground mahlepi

1/2 teaspoon masticha (crushed with 1 teaspoon sugar before adding)

11/2 cups warm milk

150 grams unsalted butter, warmed

2 heaped tablespoons dry yeast

1 cup caster sugar

3 large eggs (or 4 small eggs)

Glaze

1 egg yolk, beaten, plus 2 tablespoons of milk for glazing the top of the bread

1/4 cup flaked blanched almonds for decorating the top (optional)

Method

Pre-heat the oven to a low temperature.

In a small saucepan warm the milk.

In a bowl, place the sifted flour, salt, mahlepi and masticha. Mix and make a well in the centre, and add the yeast and 1 tablespoon of sugar to the dry ingredients.

Add only 1/2 cup of the warm milk into the well and allow the yeast to ferment. Stir gently until it bubbles.

Using the same small saucepan containing the remaining warm milk, add the butter and remainder of the sugar. Return to a low heat and continue to stir until the sugar is dissolved. Allow to cool slightly.

To the yeast mixture add the warmed milk, butter and sugar mixture, and stir to combine. Add the beaten eggs and mix well.

Knead for 10-15 minutes until the dough becomes malleable. Place the dough into a bowl that has been brushed with a little melted butter, cover with a clean cloth and place into the warmed oven to rise until doubled in size.

Punch down the dough and place onto a floured surface. Continue to knead lightly until the dough is smooth.

Divide the dough into 3 equal portions, then divide again into 3 balls. Roll each ball out to the same length, line them up and begin to plait the dough.

Place the dough into greased, oblong loaf tins. Cover with a clean cloth and leave the plaits to rise in a warm place until doubled in size.

Glaze the plaits with beaten egg yolk and milk mixture, and sprinkle with flaked almonds.

Place into the preheated oven set at 170-180 degrees, and bake for approximately 30-45 minutes. Cool on a wire rack

Roast Lamb

The Greek recipe for roast lamb is a fusion of mouthwatering aromas of lamb cooked slowly in a generous amount of olive oil, massaged with hand rubbed rigani, sprinkled with salt and pepper, infused with slivers of garlic and bathed in fresh lemon juice. Put simply; it is divine. The addition of potatoes makes for the most delicious lemon flavoured oven-roasted potatoes that are a perfect accompaniment to this tender melt-in-your-mouth roast that just falls off the bone

Ingredients

1 leg of lamb

2 cloves of garlic, cut into slits

1/2 cup of olive oil

4 tablespoons oregano, rubbed between hands

Salt

Pepper

2 cups hot water

4-6 potatoes, cut into 6 wedges

Juice of 2 lemons

Method

Trim any excess fat from the leg of lamb.

Cut slits into the leg of lamb and insert the garlic.

Place the lamb into a baking dish, pour over the olive oil and sprinkle with oregano. Season with salt and pepper, and massage the seasoning onto the lamb. Pour water into the baking dish.

Place in the oven and cook for 30 minutes, uncovered.

Turn the lamb over, and reduce the heat.

Place foil over the dish so that the lamb doesn't burn, and cook slowly for 1½ hours

After this time, season and add the potatoes.

Pour the lemon juice over the lamb and potatoes. Cover again and cook for a further 1 1/2 hours, or until the lamb is tender and the potatoes are cooked.

ΜΕΓΑΛΗ ΕΒΔΟΜΑΣ ΠΑΣΧΑ
ORTHODOX PRAYER BOOK
Η ΚΑΙΝΗ ΔΙΑΘΗΚΗ

ouzo
of
plomari
1894
PLOMARI-LESVOS
PRODUCT OF GREECE
700 ml
OUZO
ΜΥΤΙΛΗΝΗΣ

ΛΗΝΙΚΟΣ ΚΗΡΥΚΑΣ
HERAL
LARGEST NATIONAL GREEK DAILY NEWSPA
Printed & Published by F.I. PRESS
PRINT POST PUBLICATION NUMBER
Email: greek@foreignlanguage.com.au
www.greekherald.com.au
SATURDAY
22 JUNE
2013
0 680569 563798
δαίες πολιτικές εξελίξεις

The Feast of St. George

The official name day celebration for St. George falls on the 23rd of April, unless this happens to occur during the period of the Great Lent observed before Easter. If this name day does fall during Lent, celebrations will happen on the first Monday after Easter Sunday when the official church service takes place.

At the conclusion of the Easter Saturday midnight Resurrection Service the priest will usually wish a "Happy Name Day" to all those named George. My husband's name is George, and over the years we have often celebrated his name day in the traditional way by hosting a dinner for our families and friends, especially when it falls outside of Lent.

Saturday of the Souls

Psihosavato

There are several days in the Orthodox calendar known as Saturday of the Souls or Psihosavato, which fall during the Saturday of Meatfare Week, the first and second Saturdays of Great Lent, and the Saturday before Pentecost.

It is customary to devote prayers for departed relatives and loved ones, and to light a kandili (memorial lamp) in remembrance of their spirit. Families usually visit the cemetery to place flowers and light the memorial candle.

Pentecost

The Pentecost service celebrates the descent of the Holy Spirit upon the Twelve Apostles, and is conducted on the seventh Sunday after the Easter Resurrection Service (which is also the fiftieth day after Easter). Pentecost is derived from the ancient Greek word Penticosti, literally meaning 'the fiftieth day'.

Pentecost is seen as the birthday of the Christian church and is celebrated for a week. Fasting is not allowed.

All Saints Day

The first Sunday after the Pentecost is the Feast of All Saints and is a time to reflect on the saints that gave themselves to the faith. Although there are many formal individual saint days that are celebrated throughout the year, All Saints Day allows us to commemorate the life and martyrdom of both the known and unknown saints.

May Day

In Greece the 1st of May is a traditional springtime holiday known as May Day, and is a special celebration of the new spring growth after winter. Flowers are picked from the home gardens and the countryside, and beautiful floral garlands are prepared for hanging on the front gate or door.

I have fond memories as a young girl of picking flowers with my paternal grandmother and making a garland to place around my neck.

Yiayia Lambrini and I had walked a distance from the village to a small hill, and with a little basket in hand we picked fresh flowers as we came across them. Later at the family homestead we picked fresh chamomile flowers for drying and to use as a herbal tea. I remember the never-ending springtime blue sky, warm sun and fresh air as I skipped back into the village ahead of my grandmother, proudly wearing my garland. I couldn't wait for my cousins to see my beautiful floral necklace.

The 1st of May also marks the International Labour Movement's demand for the eight hour working day. Demonstrations are held in many countries and in Greece it is a public holiday named Ergatiki Protomayia. My father sang this little verse to me.

Greek Verse	English translation
Proto mayia ta louloudia yiortasoun,	*On the first of may the flowers are celebrated*
Kai ta poulia to tergia tous foliazoun.	*And the birds find their mate*
Tragoudon 'to mai hriso mai me oles tous droses'.	*They sing 'May golden May with all the morning dew'*

Panayias

August 15th is an important celebration in the Orthodox calendar. It is the celebration of the Dormition (falling asleep) of the Virgin Mary and in Greece this day marks a significant public holiday. It is usual for people to return to their family homes and reunite in celebration with their extended family.

Many families attend church on this day and although it marks the end of her earthly life, it is also the day that the Virgin Mary is reunited with her son in heaven, and therefore is a day of great celebration. Churches and monasteries hold special services and festivals to mark the occasion.

In preparation for this feast day it is usual to observe the fasting rituals from the 1st to the 14th of August in readiness to celebrate on the 15th of August. Those named Panayioti, Panayiota, Mary, Maria, and Mario celebrate their name day on this day.

My mother celebrated her name day on this day, and Dad enjoyed spoiling Mum and taking her out to lunch after attending the church service. We would usually visit Mum at home and enjoy some lovely coffee and homemade biscuits.

October

Ohi Day

At 3AM on the 28th of October 1940, in response to the ultimatum made by forces wanting to access Greece during World War II, Prime Minister Metaxas of Greece delivered an heroic, "OHI!" ("NO!"). With most of Europe having fallen, Prime Minister Metaxas knew only too well that this response meant that Greece would be invaded.

Hellenism had given the world freedom of speech and democracy. These were not values shared by the invading forces. Expressing the "OHI!" response was an heroic act of standing up for the ancient beliefs that underpinned Greek culture and history.

In Greece, this day is a public holiday and many Greeks put a Greek flag on their window as a mark of patriotism. Greek communities commemorate this day with a morning church service, followed by military parades and students marching in their blue and white uniforms or national costumes.

φιλοσοφια

Philosophy

"It is possible to fail in many ways…
while to succeed is possible only in one way."

Aristotle

25th December

Christmas is always such a special time of the year. As far back as I can remember we have always had our one family Christmas tree that is put up each year and decorated with the same beautiful ornaments. The decorations would now be classified as vintage, almost antique. I remember Mum unfurling a roll of cotton wool, then taking small tufts and placing them on the end of the branches to resemble snow. We loved decorating the tree and placing the angel at the top. At night time when we were tucked up in bed, we would leave our bedroom door ajar so that the Christmas lights would project colourful shadows onto our bedroom wall.

As is customary, a thorough cleaning and tidying of the house is performed. Greeks decorate their homes according to the seasons, and because Christmas is celebrated in the northern winter, the best linen is on display and the home's summer décor is packed away and replaced with winter décor; the woollen rugs, runners and flokatis mats are placed back onto the floor, providing extra warmth and comfort. The fine cut-out lace embroidery is replaced with heavier tapestry and needlepoint runners and doylies made of thicker yarn and providing a warmer ambience. The Christmas tree is usually put up and decorated on Christmas Eve and left up until the Epiphany on the 5th of January. Those celebrating their name day on St. John's, January 7th, will leave the tree and decorations up until January 8th.

It is usual to observe a fasting period prior to Christmas, traditionally commencing on the 15th of November. In these busy modern times, many people observe just three days of fasting before Christmas, avoiding meat, eggs, dairy products and oil. Communion is then taken on Christmas morning, in time for the Christmas luncheon feast.

The period of time between December 25th and the day of the Epiphany, January 6th, is called Dodekaemeron (twelve feasting days) and is considered to be one continuous festive period. This feasting period is also known as The Twelve Days of Christmas, and many celebrations and sharing of home-baked goodies is done during this time. As it is the holiday season, it is usual to visit friends and family and in turn receive visitors. Much socialising and celebrating is enjoyed at this festive time of the year.

At Christmas time children sing Kalanda (Christmas carols) as they visit homes in their neighbourhood. Usually they gather in small groups accompanied by the sounds of the triangle, accordion, lyre and guitar as they door knock spreading the Christmas cheer. People donate a few coins to the children for good luck or offer them special treats, or small gifts. The generosity of the Christmas spirit is very much enjoyed.

Homemakers are busy during the week preceding Christmas, baking delicious traditional biscuits and bread. These include the delightful Melamakarona (honey and walnut biscuits) infused with cinnamon, cloves, orange rind and honey, and the melt-in-your-mouth delicate Kourambiedes (almond crescent shortbread) traditionally prepared for the New Year. The welcoming aroma of baking permeates the home and adds an extra cosiness at this special time of year. Although traditionally Kourambiethes were prepared for the New Year, today it is acceptable to serve both Melamakarona and Kourambiedes during the Christmas season. Platters piled high with these delicacies are placed safely away from the temptation of little hands.

In Zakynthos it is a tradition to serve Avgolemono (egg and lemon) soup on Christmas day, and my mother continued this tradition when we were growing up making her famous thick and creamy Avgolemono from a home made rich chicken stock, with rice added until cooked. The soup was then finished with the traditional egg and lemon sauce, just before serving.

Today our large extended family follows this wonderful tradition, much to the surprise of our family friends. Avgolemono soup is followed by roast turkey seasoned with marjoram, and potatoes ladorigani (oil and oregano) served with a squeeze of fresh lemon juice. Our Christmas lunch always features Christopsomo (home-made Christmas bread) that is infused with the heady aroma of aniseed and decorated with a dough motif of the cross for placing on top of the bread before baking. Dessert consists of the traditional Kourambiedes, Melamakarona, Finikia, and seasonal fresh fruit platters. Finally a cup of Greek coffee is enjoyed and makes a perfect end to a delightful Christmas celebration.

Leading up to Christmas, the traditional greeting is, “Kala Christouyenna”, meaning “Good Christmas” or “Kales Yiortes” meaning “Happy Celebrations”. On Christmas Day the greeting is,“Chronia Polla”, meaning “Many Years”.

Those named Christos, Christine, Manolis, Manos, Emanuel or Emmanuela celebrate their name day on Christmas Day. Friends and family greet them with the customary wishes of “Hronia Polla”.

Kourambiedes

Almond Crescent Shortbread

Kourambiedes are delicious crescent-shaped shortbread covered in loose icing sugar. They are a delicacy served in most Greek homes and are a favourite treat, especially at this festive time of the year.

The blanched almonds provide a wonderful texture and the Ouzo, Cognac or Masticha provides a delightful and delicious aroma. Kourambiedes keep very well in a tin lined with baking paper; that is if you can resist the temptation to have more than one at a time!

Ingredients

250 grams unsalted butter, at room temperature

2 tablespoons sunflower oil or light extra virgin olive oil

2 tablespoons icing sugar, sifted

2 tablespoons caster sugar

1 egg yolk

1/2 cup blanched slivered almonds, toasted and chopped

3 cups self-raising flour

3 tablespoons Ouzo (substitute with Cognac or Mastiha)

Method

Preheat the oven to 180 degrees.

Place the butter, icing sugar and caster sugar into a large bowl, and beat together until the butter becomes pale and creamy. Add the oil, and continue to beat until combined.

Add the egg yolk and liqueur of choice, and mix well.

Sift into the mixture the flour, and add the toasted almonds.
Use a wooden spoon to mix until well combined.

Knead to bind the mixture together.

Take approximately 2 teaspoons of the mixture and form a ball and then slightly roll between the palms of your hands to form a small log shape. Place on the baking tray, slightly turn the ends to form a crescent and pinch each end to form a small dent.

Bake for 20 minutes until golden.

Remove from the oven and allow to cool for just a few minutes.

Place the biscuits onto a sheet of baking paper that has been dusted with icing sugar. Dust liberally with more icing sugar so that the biscuits appear to be covered in white snow.

Arrange on a serving plate, or store in a glass, airtight dish.

Melamakarona

Honey and Walnut Biscuits

Melamakarona are traditional Christmas biscuits. Their unique flavour comes from the various spices, including freshly-grated nutmeg and cinnamon, blended with the orange zest and baked to perfection. The honey syrup provides a little extra sweetness and the walnuts provide a wonderful texture. It is customary to serve Melamakarona at Christmas time but today homemakers enjoy serving them at other special occasions too.

Ingredients

1 1/2 cups sunflower oil

3/4 cup sugar

1 cup orange juice

1 cup fine semolina

5 cups self-raising flour, approximately

1 1/2 teaspoons baking soda

1 teaspoon ground nutmeg

2 teaspoons ground cinnamon

Zest of 1 orange

Syrup

1 cup water

3/4 cup sugar

1/4 cup honey

1 cinnamon stick

3 whole clove buds

Thin slice of citrus rind

Method

Preheat the oven to 200 degrees.

Beat together the oil, sugar, citrus zest and orange juice.

Add the spices, semolina and baking powder.

Add the flour a little at a time, and gently knead to form a dough.

Take a walnut sized piece of dough, and form into oval shapes, pinching both ends to a blunt point.

Decorate the top of the biscuit with 5 diagonal lines using the tines of a fork.

Bake for approximately 30 minutes, or until the biscuits are firm and golden brown.

Syrup

Place all ingredients into a pot and bring to the boil, stirring constantly.

Decoration

Crushed walnuts to sprinkle on top of the biscuits.

When completely cooled, dip 3-4 biscuits at a time into the hot syrup. Leave for 5-10 seconds, then dip the top of each biscuit into the crushed walnuts. Lift out onto a wire rack to cool.

Stuffed Finikia

Spice-Filled Biscuits

These delicious biscuits are similar to Melamakarona, the main difference being that these are stuffed with a spicy and aromatic cinnamon and nut mixture. Finikia were Mum's specialty, and her favourite way of preparing them was to sprinkle coconut on top after dipping them into the warm syrup.

Ingredients

1 cup sunflower oil

1/2 cup butter

3 tablespoons sugar

1/2 cup orange juice

1 egg, well beaten

2 teaspoons baking powder

1 teaspoon cinnamon

3 1/2 to 4 cups plain flour, sifted

Filling

1 cup chopped walnuts

2 teaspoons cinnamon

2 tablespoons honey

2 teaspoons orange juice

Syrup

2 cups sugar

2 cups water

1 cup honey

2 tablespoons lemon juice

Method

Preheat the oven to 180 degrees.

With an electric mixer, beat the oil, butter, sugar and orange juice until thoroughly blended.

Add beaten egg, baking powder, cinnamon, and enough flour to form a soft dough.

Pinch off pieces of dough the size of a walnut and flatten in the palm of the hand.

Prepare the filling by combining the nuts, cinnamon and sugar, and moistening with honey to form a thick paste.

Place 1/4 teaspoon of the nut mixture into the center of the dough.

Bring the sides in to cover the nut mixture, pinch the ends to completely seal the mixture into the biscuit. Then form into an oval shape.

Bake for 20 to 25 minutes or until golden. Cool.

Make the syrup by combining the sugar and water, and cook for 20 minutes.

Add the honey and lemon juice, and simmer for 5 minutes

Dip the biscuits into the simmering syrup, a few at a time, for 2 - 3 minutes, then roll in the ground walnuts or sprinkle with dessicated coconut.

Love and Other Ceremonies

Loggo

New love is always exciting and full of promise. As is usual in many other cultures, it is an important part of the Greek culture that the man asks the girl's parents for her hand in marriage. Essentially this request formalises the intention of the new groom-to-be and seals a promise of love, respect, honour and trust for the bride-to-be and her family.

With the parents blessing, the man proposes to the girl. The proposal is announced to family first and then friends, and plans are made for the two families to meet, usually at a lunch or dinner held at the girl's family home.
This seals the promise and makes it a little more formal.

φιλοσοφια

Philosophy

"At the touch of love everyone becomes a poet."

Plato

Engagement

Becoming engaged is one of the most beautiful events in a couple's life and is a ceremony that is conducted usually at the girl's family home, with close family and friends present. Having the family priest officiate the informal service is optional, although usually preferred.

The man is expected to have already asked the girl's father for her hand in marriage prior to the proposal and Loggo, the first coming together of the couple's respective families.

Choosing an engagement ring is a wonderful experience, and today many couples spend much time either choosing just the right ring for the occasion, or designing a ring that is personal and special. As is customary, the engagement ring is a gift from the man to his bride-to-be as a symbol of undying love. The couple also chooses their wedding bands at this time, as they will be required for the engagement ceremony.

The engagement commences with the couple, the parents and the best man or matron of honour gathering around an icon as the priest officiates and reads prayers whilst blessing the engagement and wedding rings. He also bestows blessings on the newly engaged couple. The wedding rings are placed on the left hand ring finger of the betrothed, and when the wedding ceremony takes place the wedding rings are eventually worn on the right hand. The engagement ring is then presented to the bride and worn on her right hand.

Usually the parents of the couple will adorn their respective future daughter-in-law and son-in-law with a piece of jewellery to honour the occasion.

Guests wish the couple, "Kala Stephana", which literally translates to "Good Crowns". This actually means 'may you have a good marriage', and is symbolic of the crowns placed on the heads of the bride and groom at the wedding service.

Alternatively they may say, "Ora Kali", which literally translates to "May the good hour for the marriage come".

Naturally, and as would be expected, an engagement is a wonderful opportunity for celebration and festivities, and for families and friends to gather together to witness, share and celebrate the union of the betrothed.

Krevati

Dressing of the Bridal Bed

The Greek custom of the Krevati, known as the Dressing of the Bridal Bed, is performed during the week leading up to the wedding. It is a very special custom indeed, and a good excuse for family members to gather at the bride and groom's future home to commence the celebrations.

The bridesmaids and female family members assemble in the bedroom, around the bare mattress and bed. Using a needle and red cotton thread, four young women will each proceed to sew a cross onto the corner of the mattress. When this has been completed, the bed is fully dressed with an underlay, base sheet, top sheet, bedspread and pillows. The bride's mother, as part of her trousseau, usually supplies these in the highest possible quality that one can afford. It is a way of ensuring that her daughter will want for nothing and will have exceptional quality linen that is not only beautiful, but also long-lasting.

A clean white sheet or small, white embroidered tablecloth is placed over the centre of the dressed bed to protect the linen, prior to the women sprinkling rice, rose petals, sugared almonds, and gold and silver coins on to the bed. Then a small baby boy or baby girl is placed on the bed. As is usual in Greek customs, the babies are symbols of fertility and the rice, rose petals, sugared almonds, gold and silver are to bestow blessings for richness and prosperity upon the young couple.

At the conclusion of this time-honoured ceremony, the guests partake in the hospitality that has been provided by the bride's family.

Prika

Trousseau

A special and significant custom is that of a mother providing a trousseau to her daughter. Usually this special assembly would include items lovingly prepared by the bride's mother; beautiful crisp linen, embroidered tablecloths, hand-crocheted doilies, tapestries, handmade lace, bath towels, bedspreads, pillowslips, napery, the finest china, a formal cutlery service and the best quality cookware and bakeware.

Of special significance is the passing on of family heirlooms, icons and other pieces of great sentimental value. This is such a beautiful practice that honours the relationship a mother has with her daughter. It is an elegant and deeply meaningful act of passing on valuable advice, practical tips and time-honoured traditions, taking from the past to live in the present and look to the future. It is a circle of love in the most beautiful form.

Preparing for the Wedding

A mother's pride and joy is often wrapped up in the love she has for her daughter. It is befitting then for a mother to take part in the dressing of the bride and it is usually the last act of love a mother can show her daughter before she takes her step towards a life to be shared with the one she has chosen to marry.

On the morning of the wedding, the bride's family gathers at the family home and helps prepare for the day ahead. Drinks are served, music is played, and frivolity and celebration abound.

If the bride has sisters, then together with the bridesmaids and matron of honour, they will all help with the dressing of the bride.

After the bride has been dressed, the family gathers for a dance, usually with the bride at the lead with her parents and grandparents, and other family members such as aunts, uncles and cousins.

Photographs are taken, the cars arrive, and the bride will leave her family home on the arm of her father who will present her to the groom who is patiently waiting at the church. (Of course it is considered bad luck for the groom to see the bride before the ceremony, and naturally the bride will arrive just that little bit late...)

The Best Man or Matron of Honour

Being chosen as a best man or matron of honour is not to be taken lightly. It is an important role and one that is usually fulfilled by someone extremely close to the bride and groom. Importantly, this person must also be of Orthodox faith, as they will be honoured with being the godparent of the first-born child.

This chosen person will not only be integral to the events surrounding the engagement and wedding, but will also be one of the key witnesses to these special moments. They will help celebrate the upcoming marriage, provide counsel, lend an ear, calm the groom, and ensure that he arrives at church on time. It is their duty to make sure that the wedding day unfolds smoothly.

The best man or matron of honour also provides the essential items required to conduct a Greek Orthodox marriage ceremony; this includes two large candles decorated with white linen, tulle or organza, a silver tray lined with specially selected fabric for the bride to have a dress made from after the wedding, the crowns used in the ceremony, a bottle of sweet wine for taking sips from the common cup, a sprinkling of sugared almonds, and a small gift for the couple.

The Wedding Service

The Orthodox wedding service is an ancient and beautiful ceremony filled with symbolism. It is very different in that the bride and groom do not exchange wedding vows during the ceremony. It is assumed that their presence together in the church, in front of their family and friends, means they are entering the marriage willingly.

Traditionally, the groom awaits the bride at the altar holding her flower bouquet that he will present to the bride when she arrives. After entering the church on the arm of her father, the bride is presented to her future husband. The groom respectfully kisses the hand of his father-in-law and then presents the flowers to the bride. The bride and groom turn to face the priest, who is ready to officiate the marriage.

Service of Betrothal

The candles have been lit and are held by a young relative or friend of the bride and groom.

This part of the service focuses around the exchanging of the rings. It is traditional that an Orthodox wedding is a double ring ceremony. The priest performs the betrothal service by holding the wedding rings in his right hand and blessing them by making the sign of the cross three times on the forehead of the bride and groom. Certain rituals are repeated three times as this symbolizes the Holy Trinity of the Father, Son and Holy Spirit.

The rings are then handed to the best man (Koumbaro) or matron of honour (Koumbara) who then proceeds to place them on the third fingers of the bride and groom's right hands. The exchanging of wedding rings symbolizes eternal love and devotion.

Ceremony of the Sacrament of Marriage

During this part of the service, known as the Stepsis (the Crowning), the priest will join the right hands of the bride and groom. This symbolizes the couple's union and oneness, and their hands will remain joined until the end of the wedding ceremony.

The Crowning

The crowning is a beautiful and symbolic part of the wedding service where the bride and groom are united by wedding crowns, known as Stefana. Traditionally crowns were made from orange blossom, intertwined and joined with a ribbon. Today crowns are usually made of white satin that has been plaited or intertwined, beautifully adorned with silk flowers and pearl or diamante ornaments and joined together by a white satin ribbon.

The priest holds both crowns in his right hand and makes the sign of the cross over the groom's forehead, exclaiming, "The servant of God (groom's name) takes as his crown the servant of God (bride's name) in the name of the Father and the Son and the Holy Spirit. Amen." This is repeated three times.

The crowns are then held to make a sign of the cross over the bride's forehead, exclaiming, "The Servant of God (bride's name) takes as her crown the servant of God (groom's name) in the name of the Father and the Son and the Holy Spirit. Amen." This is repeated three times.

The priest then gently places the crowns on the bride and groom. The best man, standing behind the couple, crosses his hands near the head of the bride and groom and then takes the crowns into his hands. He proceeds to cross, uncross and re-cross his hands three times over the heads of the couple, before gently returning the crowns to their heads. This crowning symbolizes that the bride and groom are the king and queen of their family.

The Common Cup

The common cup is offered to the groom and then to the bride for each to take three sips of sweet wine.
This common cup symbolizes the sharing of life together as husband and wife in harmony, through joy or sorrow.

The Ceremonial Walk

Holding the Holy Gospel in one hand and the hands of the couple in the other, the priest leads the bride and groom, who are still wearing their crowns, on a processional walk, known as The Dance of Isaiah. This is a procession repeated three times around the centre table in a circular fashion. The best man follows behind, as do the boy and girl who are holding the lit wedding candles. This ceremonial walk symbolizes the couple taking their first steps together as husband and wife.

The Removal of the Crowns

When the ceremonial walk has ended, the priest blesses the couple, the crowns are removed, and he then separates their previously joined hands with the Holy Gospel, reminding them that only God can break the union which they have just entered into.

After the ceremony

The bridal couple remains in the church to receive the good wishes from their invited family and friends.

The traditional greeting is, "Na Zisete" ("May you live a long and happy life").

Afterwards, when exiting the church, the guests throw sugar-coated almonds, rice and confetti on the happy couple.

A celebratory reception follows, with lots of food, drinking, dancing and kefi continuing late into the night.

A moving and traditional wedding song is usually played at the dressing of the bed, at the bride's home on the morning of the wedding and at the reception. It describes that a marriage is taking place in a beautiful garden, and that the mother and daughter will now be separated. It advises the groom to love his bride, to always be kind, and to admire her like the loveliness of basil that has been planted in the ground. It tells, 'Raise proud eagle and open your wings so that the partridge that is folded in your embrace may rise and take flight'.

Wedding Song

Σήμερα γάμος γίνεται
Σήμερα γά , σήμερα γάμος γίνεται
σ' ωραίο περιβόλι, σ' ωραίο περιβόλι

Σήμερα απο , σήμερα αποχωρίζεται
η μάνα από την κόρη, η μάνα από την κόρη

Γαμπρέ τη νύ , γαμπρέ τη νύφη ν' αγαπάς
Να μην την εμαλώνεις, να μην την εμαλώνεις

Σαν το βασί , σαν το βασιλικό στη γη
να τηνε καμαρώνεις, να τηνε καμαρώνεις

Σήκω περή , σήκω περήφανε αητέ
κι άνοιξε τα φτερά σου, κι άνοιξε τα φτερά σου

Να πεταχτεί, να πεταχτεί η πέρδικα
που 'χεις στην αγκαλιά σου, που 'χεις στην αγκαλιά σου

Simera gamos yinete
Se oreo perivoli, se oreo perivoli

Simera apo, simera apohorizete
I mana apo tin kori, i mana apo tin kori
Gambre ti ni, gambre ti nifi na ayapas
Na min tin emalonis, na min tin emalonis

San to vasi, san to vasiliko stin yi
Na tin e kamaronis, na tin e kamaronis

Siko peri, siko perifane aite
Ke anikse ta ftera sou, ke anikse ta ftera sou

Na petahtei, na petahtei i perthika
Pou eheis stin agalia sou, pou eheis stin agalia sou.

Wedding Bread

Kouloura tis Nifis

Greece has many bread-making traditions steeped in rich symbolism especially surrounding major feast days and the milestones of life such as engagements and weddings. The wedding breads had a particular significance for the happiness of the couple and for them to enjoy a well-fated marriage.

Traditionally the women of the groom's family bake these large round loaves or rings that represent eternity and offer them to the bride's family as a symbol of kinship. These wedding breads (kouloures tis nifis) bear a special decoration using sculpted dough motifs such as pomegranates, cypresses, grapes, crosses, birds, and flower-wreaths. It is believed that these motifs will bring good fortune to the couple and will protect them from evil.

The bread may be infused with aromatic spices such as aniseed, fennel, cinnamon and cloves and then sprinkled with walnuts and sesame seeds, and sometimes a foil wrapped coin may be placed inside for good luck.

My mother infused her Christmas bread with the heady aroma of aniseed and made a dough motif of the cross for placing on top of the bread. She then sprinkled it with sesame seeds before baking. The result was a sweetly aromatic and decorative bread that we all greatly enjoyed. It is not too dissimilar to the kouloures tis nifis that is especially found in many parts of Greece including the Ioanian island of Zakynthos where my father's family is from.

Ioanian Wedding Bread

Ingredients

4 cups special plain flour

1 1/2 tablespoons yeast

11/2 tablespoons sugar

1 1/3 cups warm water,
to be added gradually

1/2 teaspoons salt

2 tablespoons extra virgin olive oil

2 tablespoons pure honey

1 teaspoon ground fennel seed

1/2 teaspoon ground aniseed

1 large egg, lightly whisked to combine dough mixture

4 tablespoons milk,
to glaze

Decorations

Mix sifted plain flour with water until a soft dough forms.

Make shapes to place on top of dough for decoration.

Method

Preheat oven to low.

In a small bowl, combine yeast, sugar and 1/3 of a cup of warm water.

Cover with a clean cloth, place into the warm oven to activate yeast.

In a large bowl combine the flour, salt, the remainder of warm water that has been mixed with the honey, olive oil, yeast mixture, spices and egg.

Mix well and then turn the dough onto a floured surface and continue to knead for approximately 10 minutes until smooth.

Place the ball of dough in a large bowl that has been lightly greased with olive oil, and cover with a clean tea towel and place into the warm oven to rise and double in size. This should take approximately an hour or more.

Meanwhile using the additional dough, knead and roll out shapes and motifs for decorating the wedding bread. These could be birds, trees, grapevines, a house, the sun, flowers or coils and other beautiful decorative shapes.

Punch the bread dough down and continue kneading for a few minutes.

Place into a warmed baking tin, and press gently just shy from the edge of the pan. Working quickly, decorate the bread with the hand made motifs and return to warm oven to rise once again. This should take approximately 30 minutes.

Increase the temperature to 180 degrees and brush the bread dough with a little milk.

Bake approximately 30-40 minutes or until golden brown.

The bread is ready when a hollow sound is made when tapped.

If the bread is browning too quickly, cover with a sheet of aluminum foil and reduce the oven temperature slightly.

Wedding Bread

Easy Recipe

Ingredients

4 cups plain flour

1 1/2 tablespoons dry yeast

3 tablespoons sugar

1/4 of a cup of warm water

1 tablespoon salt

4 tablespoons butter

1 1/2 cups milk

ground spices if used (cinnamon, fennel, or aniseed)

decorated dough motifs, if used

4 tablespoons milk, to glaze

Method

Preheat oven to low.

Heat the milk with the butter.

In a small bowl, combine yeast, 1 teaspoon of sugar and 1/4 of a cup of warm water.

Cover with a clean cloth, place into the warm oven to activate yeast.

In a large bowl combine the salt, sugar, half the flour and any spices if used.

Add the yeast mixture and knead adding the rest of the flour slowly until the dough no longer sticks to the hands.

Shape the dough into a loaf or a kouloura (doughnut) and decorate with motifs if desired.

Place the dough on to a lightly oiled baking tray and cover with a cloth.

Return the tray to the warm oven and allow the dough to rise until it doubles in size.

Turn up the heat to 190 degrees and brush the bread dough with a little milk.

Bake 50 -60 minutes or until golden brown.

The bread is ready when a hollow sound is made when tapped.

If the bread is browning too quickly, cover with a sheet of aluminum foil and reduce the oven temperature slightly.

Diples are a dessert originating from the Peloponese. These delightful sweets are made from thinly rolled out dough that is cut intro strips, and folded whilst being deep-fried. The result is a delicate and delicious sweet treat that is then drizzled with pure honey and sprinkled with ground cinnamon, granulated sugar, and chopped walnuts. Traditionally diples are served at weddings, baptisms and other celebrations.

Ingredients

3 eggs

2 tablespoons sugar

1/4 cup orange juice

2 tablespoons brandy

1 1/2 teaspoons pure vanilla essence, optional

1 teaspoons baking powder

2 cups plain flour, approximately

Sunflower oil for frying

Topping

Pure honey

Ground cinnamon

Granulated sugar

Ground walnuts

Method

Sift the flour and baking powder into a bowl.

In a separate large bowl beat the eggs until pale and creamy. Add the sugar and continue to beat until dissolved.

Add the orange juice, brandy and vanilla essence and beat well.

Add the sifted flour and knead the dough until smooth, and then divide the dough into 5 equal pieces. Cover with a clean tea towel and set aside to rest.

Roll each piece of dough out into thin, long strips.

Cut each strip into individual pieces approximately 5 inches x 3 inches and place onto a large platter separated by kitchen paper to prevent them from sticking together.

Pour approximately 3-4 inches of sunflower oil into a frying pan, and heat.

Place a piece of dough into the hot oil and working quickly, with two forks, roll the dough into a loosely folded scroll. Fry until light golden brown. Remove from pan and drain onto absorbent kitchen paper.

Transfer to a serving platter and cool.

To store, cover with absorbent paper and then cover with a clean tea towel.

To serve, take the number of diples required, drizzle in honey, and sprinkle with cinnamon, granulated sugar and ground walnuts.

Diples may also be dipped into syrup made from honey, sugar and water just before serving.

Anna
Mary

Births and Baptisms

The anticipation of the birth of a child is an exciting and heartwarming occasion. Of course grandparents are waiting to dote on the newborn, and parents are happy and nervous about the arrival of a baby.

It is traditional to bestow good luck on a newly born baby. Visitors place silver and gold coins into the crib so that the child is blessed with strength and prosperity. A ball of cotton wool may also be placed into the crib. This resembles the white hair of an aged person, so in effect the wish being bestowed is that of long life.

After the birth, the priest can also be invited to bless the mother and the baby. The baby will then receive its official name day blessing on the eighth day.

A little gold religious pin (filahtiko) or a small icon of the Mother Mary and baby Jesus may be placed on or above the crib to overlook and to protect the baby.

It is usual for mothers to stay at home with their baby for the first forty days after birth. This helps the mum develop a good routine for herself, with good nutrition and rest, and to keep the baby safe, warm and comfortable.

Sarantisi Blessing

Forty day blessing of a baby

A special and meaningful tradition is to Sarantisi a baby. Saranta is the Greek word for the number forty. The Sarantisi blessing is the bestowing of a personal blessing on the mother and child on or around forty days after the birth. An appointment is made with the parish priest as the blessing is usually a stand-alone event that can occur at any time during the week, and only takes a few minutes to conduct. This is a private and personal service and is usually attended by the grandmothers. From this point the baby can be brought to church and taken on outings.

Nursery Rhymes

Sung to the tune of To the tune of 'See-Saw Margery Daw

Κούνια - μπέλα έπεσ' η κοπέλα χτύπησε το γόνα της και φωνάζει η νόνα της.	*Kounyia bella Epese I kopela, Htipise to yona tis Kai fonazi tin nona tis.*	*Swinging - pretty one The little girl fell off the swing, She hurt her knee And her grandmother is shouting.*

Lullaby

Νάνι ,νάνι ,νάνι ,νάνι Το μωράκι μου να κάνει Ύπνος στα ματάκια του Νάνι του να κοιμηθεί Και καλα να σηκωθεί	*Nani, nani, nani, nani To moraki mou na kanei Ipne sta matakia tou Nani tou na koimithi Kai kala to sikothi.*	*Sleep, sleep sleep, sleep My little baby will sleep Sleepy little eyes Sleep to a sweet lull And then to wake up*

φιλοσοφια

Philosophy

"Children are the anchors that hold a mother to life."

Sophocles

Becoming a godparent is a most significant event in the life of a person of Greek Orthodox faith. The love and protection of the child is of paramount importance, and the godparent must be a guiding light and teacher of spiritually and faith. As well as spoiling the child at birthdays and Christmas, this special relationship between a godchild and its godparents is much revered, and is considered a lifelong commitment.

The godparents have much preparation to attend to prior to a baptism, and certain traditions are observed; these include the preparation of a baptismal box that will contain a small bottle of olive oil, a sheet, a bath towel, a small hand towel and cake of soap, singlet, nappy, socks, baptismal gown, dress or suit, coat and bonnet, shoes, rattle, icon and one full-length candle decorated with tulle or linen and adorned with flowers. This candle represents the eternal light and is lit at the commencement of the service.

The godparents also select a cross and necklace for the child to keep, and it is usually in yellow gold or white gold. This will be placed onto the child during the baptismal ceremony. Bonboniere will be selected and purchased by the godparent and given out to guests at the reception. Sometimes upon entering the church the godparent might provide small baptismal pins and these are placed on the lapels of the guests as they arrive.

A child's baptismal day is one of the most important days in the life of an Orthodox person, and the baptism occurs in the first year of the baby's life. The parents' best man or matron of honour is usually bestowed with the privilege of baptizing the firstborn child.

Godparents take on a very important role and are considered to be second parents who have the responsibility for nurturing and guiding their young charges.

The baptism is officiated at the church, and the godparent and the priest wait for the parents and baby at the entrance of the Church.

The parents hand the baby to the godparent and the priest continues to read prayers and begins blessing the child. The priest recites the prayer "I Believe In One God" and the godparent is prompted to show their support and confirmation during this reading by repeating the entire creed as the sponsor of the child. The congregation sits patiently inside and waits for the priest to lead the godparent, holding the baby, into the church ready to witness this special sacrament.

A change table is provided and the baby is undressed. A white sheet is placed over the godparent's shoulder to help protect their clothing and the baby is handed to the godparent who holds them closely. The priest blesses the water of the baptismal font and adds olive oil provided by the godparent.

The godparent hands the baby to their assisting relative to remove the clothing. The baby is then returned to the godparent who holds the baby whilst the priest proceeds to make the sign of the cross over certain parts of the baby with the olive oil. The priest proceeds to hold the baby over the font whilst the godparent covers the baby in olive oil. The priest then immerses the baby in the baptismal font three times whilst reciting prayers and the baby's Christian name, which traditionally is the name of the grandmother or grandfather, or other family name.

The baby is annointed with Holy Myron which is a special oil made only every ten years in Constantinople. The priest makes the sign of the cross, and then proceeds to cut four tiny pieces of hair in the shape of a cross on the child's head. The singlet is placed on the baby, the cross and chain provided by the godparents is blessed and the priest places the cross over the baby's head. Finally the priest hands the baby back to the godparent, and the baby is returned to the change table and dressed in the new clothes that have been especially chosen for the occasion.

At the end of the ceremony the mother proceeds to the icon of Mary, kisses it and makes the sign of the cross three times followed by a curtsey. The mother approaches the godparent to kiss their hand prior to that of the priest, before eagerly receiving the newly baptised child into her arms. The parents and godparents and immediate family then line up at the altar to receive the guests' good wishes.

The customary greeting to the parents of the baby is, "Na sas Zisei" ("Long life to your baby"), and to the godparents it is, "Panta Axia", which translates to "May you always be worthy".

The ceremony is followed by a celebration at the family's house, a hall or a restaurant where guests receive sugar-coated almond bonboniere to commemorate this special occasion.

After the Baptism

There are a number of traditions surrounding bathing and communion to be observed after a baby's baptism.

Because the baby has been anointed with Holy Myron the parents should not bathe the child by immersion into a water bath for three days following the baptism.

On the third evening the godparents give the baby its first bath in a baby bathtub. Importantly because the bath water contains Holy Myron, the water is not left to drain down the sink, but instead is used to water trees and shrubs in the garden. Separately, all garments that the baby has worn since its baptism are carefully and gently washed in a bucket or baby bathtub, and again the water is used to water shrubs and trees.

The parents and godparents devote the following three Sundays to taking the baby to church to receive Holy Communion. It is customary for the baby to be dressed in full baptismal attire and for the baptismal candle to be lit prior to the baby being administered communion.

In my family we celebrated our girls' communion and honoured the godparents with a shared lunch with our respective parents.

Name Days

Most Greeks are given religious names and celebrate their name day on the same day as the appropriate saint. Name days are considered to be more important than birthdays, and it is usual for people to receive gifts on their name day.

Adults celebrate with small parties. The host or hostess prepares an assortment of savoury food called mezedes and offers visitors drinks such as beer, brandy, ouzo, or other liqueurs, followed by an assortment of homemade cakes and biscuits served with Greek coffee. The usual greeting is, "Hronia Polla" ("Many Years").

Some of the popular name days are:

Jan 1st	*Basil*
Jan 6th	*Foti and Fotini*
Jan 7th	*John*
January 17th	*Anthony*
January 18th	*Athanssios*
January 25th	*Gregory*
March 7th	*Alex*
March 25th	*Evangelia or Evangelos*
March 25th	*Mark*
April 23rd	*George*
May 5th	*Irene*
May 21st	*Constantine and Helen*
June 16th	*Matthew*
June 9th	*All Saints Day*
June 29th	*Peter and Paul*
July 7th	*Kyriaki*
July 17th	*Olga*
July 20th	*Elias*
July 24th	*Christine*
August 15th	*Mary, Maria, Panayiota and Panayioti*
August 27th	*Fanourios*
September 1st	*Aspasia, Athina, Aphrodite, Antigone, Penelope, and Margarita*
October 18th	*Luke*
October 23rd	*James*
November 8th	*Michael and Gabriel*
November 25th	*Catherine*
November 30th	*Andrew*
December 5th	*Savvas*
December 6th	*Nicholas*
December 9th	*Anna*
December 12th	*Spyridon*
December 17th	*Daniel*
December 22nd	*Anastasia*
December 24th	*Eugenia*
December 25th	*Chris, Emanuel*
December 26th	*Steven, Stephen, Stephanie*

**Anastasi and Anastasia, Lambros and Lambrini are celebrated on Holy Saturday after the resurrection service

Μακρινίτσα

Death and Mourning

There are many traditions and rituals surrounding death and mourning in the Greek Orthodox faith. It is usual to consult with the local priest and other relatives to ensure that the traditions are followed appropriately.

The Greek Orthodox religion believes in eternal life, therefore cremation is forbidden. The church emphasizes that the deceased is with God, so death is believed to only be the separation of the soul from the body. A new physical body will be reunited with the soul at the Last Judgement.

If a person is close to death, the family will usually invite a priest to administer sacraments, offer communion and observe confession. Often this can provide immense comfort both to the dying and their family.

φιλοσοφια

Philosophy

"The art of living well and the art of dying well are one."

Epicurus

Gracious Offers of Help

Help is so generously offered by those close to the family at this time of grief. People naturally reach out to comfort and bring food for the family. This is to feed not just the body, but also to nourish the soul and sustain energy during this difficult time. Sharing loss is of immense value in dealing with grief.

When we lost our beloved Mother, our family had so many offers of help, and this eased the immediate needs. As tradition dictates, family friends brought bottles of brandy, jars of coffee and plates of homemade paximathia (fasting biscuits) that helped us be prepared to serve guests as they arrived.

A close family friend offered to teach my sisters and sisters-in-law the skills required to prepare for this time. She took us under her wing and taught us, through demonstration in her home, how to prepare the two types of bread and kolliva (wheat dish). We will be eternally grateful to this special family friend for sharing her knowledge and guiding us during this time.

Another family friend explained in fine detail the process of what was required, and others offered to make the preparations on our behalf. Our choice was to learn so that we could practise the reverent customs to allow us to honour our mother – for all that she was, all that she did, and all that she means to us. I will never forget the offers of help, and I feel thankful and deeply grateful for the assistance we received.

Our mother was a much-respected matriarch in the Greek community and had offered many people help and guidance over the years, so now her good deeds were being returned. Everything had come full circle and the traditions that we knew our mother had practised were now left to us, which we undertook with reverence, solemnity, respect and love.

Mourning

The official period of mourning after the loss of a loved one is forty days. During this time relatives are dressed in all black. This indicates to outsiders that the family is in mourning, and therefore helps community members to approach the subject carefully and compassionately. The mourners do not attend social occasions, parties or celebrations through this period, nor listen to music or dance. Traditionally during the forty day period, families observe fasting rituals. Relatives may choose to be in mourning for a longer period of time, sometimes up to a year or more, and widows and widowers may wear black for the rest of their lives; it is a personal choice.

The grieving family accepts visitors into their homes from the time the announcement is made through to the day of the funeral. It is customary for visitors to bring bottles of brandy, jars of coffee, bottles of wine and special fasting dry biscuits called paximathia.

The grieving family will offer visitors a glass of brandy, followed by a Greek coffee served with a glass of water and paximathia. No sweets are served during this period of mourning.

Trisagion
Last Rites

The prayer service held by the priest just after death and in the presence of the deceased is called the Trisagion or last rites. On the night before the funeral, the Trisagion is usually held again in the chapel of a funeral home. This is also an occasion for viewing the deceased. The Trisagion is repeated again, either in church or at the cemetery, usually on the third day, the ninth day, the fortieth day, three months, six months, nine months and the one year memorial after the death.

Funeral and Burial

The family consults with the priest and arranges a suitable time for the funeral and burial to take place. It is tradition that funerals are held on weekdays and sometimes on Saturdays, but never on Sundays. A Greek Orthodox funeral stands alone and is not part of another service.

The family appoints a funeral director, and arrangements are made for the funeral and burial notices to appear in the local newspaper. Other paperwork is completed, including the death certificate.

On the day of the funeral the deceased is brought home in the coffin by a hearse, and the family gathers for a private viewing. The priest officiates and reads prayers. This is a very private time and only the closest relatives are present.

The deceased leaves the home to travel to the church, followed by the mourning family, whilst the closest friends attending the funeral service wait outside the church until the procession arrives.

As the bell tolls, the coffin is taken into the church with the family members following behind. Friends who have assembled outside the church then follow the family into the church for the service.

Usually the service can take between thirty and sixty minutes and is conducted in its entirety by the priest. At the conclusion of the service the priest delivers the eulogy and shares the life story of the deceased with the congregation. After the service, the family file one by one, followed by the attendees, to bow in front of the coffin and kiss the icon or cross that has been laid on the chest of the deceased, or on top of the coffin. The family is then seated in a straight row to accept expressions of sympathy. At the end of the funeral church service the guests assemble outside the church, and the bells ring as the coffin is carried to the hearse for delivery to the final resting place.

The coffin, followed by a procession of family members and guests, arrives at the cemetery. The immediate family members sit beside the open grave. The priest recites prayers and blesses the deceased with burning incense. The coffin is anointed with olive oil and red wine and kolliva (boiled plain wheat) prior to the priest sprinkling the coffin with earth.

At the conclusion of the burial service, the family members drop a flower onto the coffin one by one. Then the family members and guests take a handful of earth and sprinkle it over the lowered coffin as they pay their last respects. As is customary at an Orthodox funeral, a bowl of fresh water is available for the rinsing of hands prior to leaving the cemetery.

Memory Eternal Chant

Eonia i Minimi

The memory eternal chant is sung at the end of funeral services, at the burial, and at memorial services that are held at the church. Prayers are read for those who have departed and their names are announced, followed by the choir singing, "memory eternal, memory eternal, memory eternal".

Expressions of Sympathy

"Zoi se sas" ("May life be granted to you"), which is said to family members at the funeral

"Syllypitiria" ("My condolences"), which is said only at the funeral

"O Theos na ton/tin synghoresi" ("May God forgive him/her"), which is said to family members at the funeral and at memorial services

"O Theos na ton/tin anapafsi" ("May God allow him/her to rest"), which is said to family members at the funeral, memorial services and at other times.

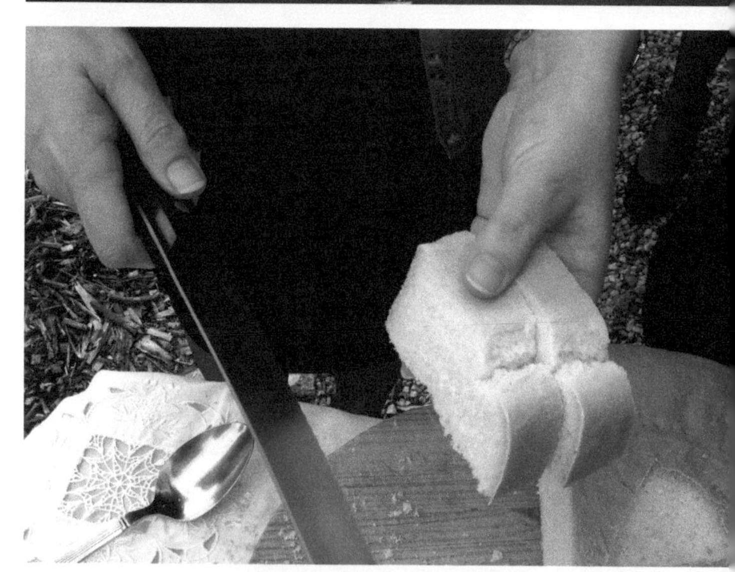

The Wake

It is customary to host a wake after the funeral. Depending on the size of the funeral, this may take place in the family home, church hall or community venue. The venue is set up for a simple fasting meal, with tables covered in white linen. Bottles of water and jugs of wine sit on the table together with small plates of paximathia.

On arrival, guests are offered a small glass of brandy. This is consumed immediately and the empty glass is then placed on a side table.

Sometimes a buffet is prepared and the guests will be given a plate to enable them to choose freely from the offerings, before proceeding to the dining tables. At other times, plates that have been pre-prepared will be provided to the guests.

The immediate family sits at the front of the hall on one long dining table covered in white cloth. A framed photo of the deceased will take pride of place at the table.

The fasting meal provided usually consists of olives, cheese, cucumber, tomato, spanakopita (spinach pie) and tiropita (cheese pie). No meat or fish is served.

Lastly, a small cup of Greek coffee is offered to have with the paximathia that are already plated at the table.

Our mother often said, “It is not possible to have a funeral without laughter, nor a wedding without tears”.

Δεν υπάρχει κηδεία χωρίς γέλιο και γάμος χωρίς κλάμα.

Memorial Services

Memorials are a significant part of the grieving process in the Greek culture. Prayers are read for forgiveness and mercy for the soul of the deceased. These memorial services are called a Mnimosyno.

Memorial services are held on the third, ninth and fortieth day memorial of the person's passing, along with recognition at three months, six months, nine months and twelve months. If the funeral occurs after the third day, then this memorial is observed at the funeral. The forty day memorial service takes place on the Sunday closest to the fortieth day after the passing, but not after the exact forty days. The memorial service is conducted at the end of a normal Sunday church service.

The immediate family members of the deceased sit in the front pews of the church. The family provides prosfero bread and a pre-prepared or pre-ordered tray of kolliva, decorated with a cross and the initials of the deceased person. These are placed on a table with candles at the front of the church.

Upon entering the church, the family members of the deceased purchase two candles. One is placed on the tray next to the kolliva, for the priest to light during the memorial for the deceased, and the other is lit by the family member at the front of the church in memory of their deceased.

The women in the immediate family of the deceased prepare two special breads. One is Artos (unleavened bread to be used at the cemetery) and the other is prosfero (unleavened bread presented as an offering to the church). Just before baking, these breads are imprinted with a special stamp called a prosfero seal that is made from either wood or plastic. It is round and is engraved with various shapes representative of the faith. Kolliva (boiled wheat, walnuts, icing sugar, cinnamon and pomegranate) is also prepared for the memorial service to be held at the cemetery.

It is essential to be serene in thought and clean in deed when following these time-honoured traditions to remember our loved ones.

φιλοσοφια

Philosophy

"Time is a doctor who heals all griefs."

Diphlus

At the Cemetery

Arrangements are made with the priest to book a time for the memorial service that is conducted at the cemetery. Notification is sent to the immediate family and close friends.

The Artos (unleavened bread) is taken to the cemetery together with the prepared kolliva on the Saturday or other designated day, prior to the Sunday memorial service.

The immediate family and closest friends assemble at the cemetery for the memorial service. This is a short fifteen minute service. The family is required to provide a small table covered with a white table cloth, bread board and bread knife, together with napkins, and bowls and spoons for serving the kolliva. A lighter will be needed to light the oil candle known as the kandili. The table is set and the Artos and kolliva are placed on it.

The special oil candle is lit, and the priest prepares the incense burner with a charcoal lighter and beads of frankincense, or other beautifully scented incense. The highly ornate incense burner is made from gold and hangs at the end of three chains that have twelve bells attached. The priest sways the incense burner to release the heady aroma as he conducts the memorial by reading special prayers for the deceased and the living family members.

After this short graveside service, the priest is given the Artos. He blesses the bread before taking a small piece for himself from the centre, the area of the bread that has been marked with the seal. The family then proceeds to cut pieces for each member attending. The kolliva is served in the small bowls together with teaspoons.

At the Sunday Memorial Church Service

A tray of kolliva is ordered from the parish for inclusion at the Sunday service on which the memorial will take place. Although homemade kolliva is preferred for the private graveside memorials, the churches prefer to have kolliva ordered from their high-quality suppliers for the Sunday service. This ensures that the wheat is fresh and free of mould or contaminants.

The prepared prosforo is wrapped in a small, white linen tablecloth or clean white tea towel, and is taken by a family member to the Sunday church service following the memorial held at the cemetery. An envelope containing a monetary donation is presented to the church as a gesture of appreciation. The name of the deceased is written on the outside, together with a symbol of a cross.

The memorial service is conducted at the end of a normal Sunday church service and is attended by the immediate family members of the deceased. The front pews of the church are dedicated to the grieving family. Friends will also attend this service to honour and remember the deceased.

Inside the church, the trays of kolliva are placed on a specially prepared table in the nave. The beautifully prepared kolliva are covered in loose icing sugar that has been firmly compounded, and cachous (edible, silver cake decorating shapes) decorate the kolliva with the initials of the deceased and other religious motifs. The priest lights the candles that have been placed beside the kolliva, and reads prayers at the end of the service for those who have departed.

At the end of the service, the kolliva are placed into a serving bowl and distributed in small paper bags to the congregation and people attending the memorial service.

Friends attending the memorial service are invited to join the family for a meal. The meal shared on this occasion is similar to the one served at the time of the funeral, and consists of olives, cheese, tomato, cucumber, bread, paximathia, wine and coffee.

Prosforo literally means 'offering', and this special bread is prepared as an offering to the church at times of memorial. It is a sacred and reverent gesture, and the one who prepares prosforo must be clean in mind, body and spirit.

It is customary to present the bread to the church as an offering together with the name of the deceased. The prosforo is blessed by the priest and during the church service, when it is time to pray for those who have passed, the priest will recite the names of the deceased. Later the prosforo is divided into small pieces as an offering (antidoron) after the congregation receives Holy Communion.

When making prosforo bread it is essential to use utensils that are exclusively dedicated to the preparation of prosforo. It is also important to keep the salt and yeast away from each other, to ensure that the salt doesn't interfere with the yeast developing. Prosforo bread does not contain any olive oil or other fats. The tin is oiled with a small piece of candle wax that has been obtained from a church candle.

Prosforo Bread

Altar Bread

Ingredients

3 cups fine milled plain flour, sifted

1/2 tablespoon of salt, placed on one side of the bowl

1 tablespoon dry yeast, placed on the other side of the bowl

1 cup warm water (added gradually)

Orthodox Religious Bread Seal

Method

Warm the oven, then turn off and place the empty tin inside to keep warm.

In a large bowl sift the flour, and add the salt and yeast to opposite sides of the bowl.

Add half of the warm water to the yeast, and mix to activate.

Gently knead the ingredients a little by hand, adding the remainder of the water as required.

Transfer the dough to a wooden board (only used for this purpose) and knead until smooth and elastic.

Remove the tin from the warm oven and coat with candle wax.

Gently place the dough in the warm tin, but do not let the dough touch the edge of the tin.

Using a clean tea towel to cover the dough, press the base of a large plate or baking dish over the tea towel to slightly flatten the dough so that it fits into the baking tin.

Stamp the dough with the religious seal and leave for 5 minutes before gently lifting.

Cover with a cloth and place in the warmed oven to rise for approximately 15-20 minutes.

When doubled in size, increase the oven temperature to 170 degrees and bake for approximately 1 hour and 5 minutes.

Remove, wrap in a large clean cloth and allow to cool

Artos Bread

This special bread is prepared at home by the family of the deceased, and is taken to the cemetery, together with the kolliva for the graveside memorial service to honour the dearly departed.

The family gathers with the priest, who recites prayers and burns incense for the repose of the soul. This service usually takes fifteen minutes, and when completed the priest cuts a small piece of the Artos for himself and then the family divides the bread up to share amongst those attending the service.

Ingredients

4 cups fine milled plain flour, sifted

1 tablespoon salt, placed on one side of the bowl

1 1/2 tablespoons dry yeast mixed, placed on the opposite side of bowl

2 tablespoons sugar, placed on the same side as the yeast

2 tablespoons olive oil, dissolved with a little warm water

2 3/4 cups of warm water, approximately - to be added gradually

4 tablespoons milk, to glaze

Method

Warm the oven, then turn off and place the empty tin inside to keep warm.

In a large bowl sift the flour, add the salt to one side of the bowl and add the yeast and sugar to the opposite side of the bowl.

Add half of the warm water to the yeast, stir to activate, and then add the olive oil.

Gently mix the ingredients with oiled hands, adding the remainder of the water as required.

Knead until smooth and elastic.

Grease the baking tin with olive oil.

Place the dough into the oiled pan, and stamp the bread with the religious seal.

Before lifting the seal, cut around the edge of the seal using a small, sharp knife.

Return the tin to the warm oven and allow to rise until the dough nearly fills the shape of the pan.

Increase the oven temperature to 180 degrees and bake for approximately 40 minutes.

Remove the bread from the baking tin and brush with milk.

Replace the bread on the oven racks and continue baking for a further 20 minutes, until the top and sides are golden brown.

Tap the bread to test if it's ready; it should sound hollow.

Kolliva

Kolliva are especially prepared for honouring those who have passed. It is recommended that the kolliva are prepared over two days. The wheat is prepared the night before and then the kolliva can be assembled and decorated the next day, using the ingredients reserved especially for this purpose.

Ingredients

250 grams clean wheat

200grams sesame seeds, dry toasted and blended to a paste

125 grams currants

125 grams blanched almonds

125 grams walnuts, roughly chopped

Small bowl of parsley, finely chopped

1/2 teaspoon ground cloves

1 teaspoon ground cinnamon

For decorating

(reserve from above)

3/4 of the sesame paste

1/4 cup currants

1/2 cup whole blanched almonds

1/4 cup chopped walnuts

Pomegranate seeds

1 cups pure icing sugar

Method

To prepare the wheat, put the kettle on and bring to the boil.

Place the wheat in a medium-sized pot and then add the hot water. Boil for 5 minutes and drain.

Rinse the wheat with hot water from the kettle.

Boil for 2 minutes and remove from heat

Leave the wheat to soak overnight.

The next morning

Drain the wheat and rinse with boiling water from the kettle.

Place the wheat over a large clean tablecloth and, using your hands, spread evenly.

Let dry for several hours. The wheat should be separate and not sticky.

Whilst the wheat is drying it is time to prepare all the other ingredients.

How to Assemble

Set aside the ingredients for decorating the kolliva.

Place all other ingredients into a medium-sized clear, glass or crystal serving bowl.

Mix carefully and press to make smooth.

Gently smooth the reserved sesame paste over the wheat mixture.

Sift the icing sugar over the sesame paste.

Using a piece of baking paper, proceed to smooth out the icing sugar using your hands. This helps compound the sugar into a smooth surface ready for decorating.

Discard the baking paper.

Decorating the Kolliva

Edge the top of the bowl with blanched almonds.

Form a cross on top with the remaining almonds and fill the 4 quadrants as follows:

1/4 with pomegranate seeds

1/4 with walnuts

1/4 with raisins

1/4 with the initials of the deceased or a flower motif using blanched almonds and a raisin in the centre.

Alternatively, use cinnamon to cover one quarter, and cachous (edible, silver cake-decorations) can be used to spell the initials of the deceased in another, or to make the shape of a cross or flower. There are endless ways in which to decorate kolliva.

φιλοσοφια

Philosophy

"What you leave behind is not what is engraved in stone monuments, but what is woven into the lives of others."

Pericles

Ikonostasis

In a traditional Greek home, there is usually a special place for the collection of icons and other religious ornaments. This collection is called an ikonostasis and may include a collection of icons, an incense burner, oil candle, prayer books and other religious items. The oil candle may be free-standing or suspended by three chains from an ornamental wall bracket.

The word iconostasis literally means 'icon stand'. This also describes the wall of religious paintings in the church that separates the nave, where the worshippers stand, from the sanctuary, which is the area around the altar.

At home there are two traditions that can be carried out for memorials and personal blessings. To conduct these, you will require a kandili and an incense burner. Most Greek shops sell kits that contain small charcoals, incense, cork floats and wicks specifically for this purpose.

Kandili

It is customary to light a kandili at home when remembering those who have passed, or for a personal blessing. When handling traditional oil lamps a great deal of care is needed. An oil lamp comes in three sections; a decorative base, a removable decorative top with cut-out motifs, and the inner glass vessel that is available in clear glass as well as red, blue and gold coloured glass.

Fill the glass vessel to the halfway mark with good quality olive oil. Thread a short wick through a cork float, and gently place onto the olive oil. Ensure that it is indeed floating, and light the wick. The flame should be a gentle flicker and not a high flame. Gently return the top to the kandili lamp and place the kandilli away from drafts, small children and pets. It is not recommended to add water to the oil (as some people do) as this will cause the oil to splatter.

ΜΕΓΑΛΗ ΕΒΔΟΜΑΣ ΠΑΣΧΑ
ORTHODOX PRAYER BOOK
Η ΚΑΙΝΗ ΔΙΑΘΗΚΗ

Incense Burner

Incense burners are used at home to conduct personal blessings. The burners are beautifully ornamental and are mostly available in gold or silver. The base is solid and the top has ornamental cut-out patterns to allow the incense to release its beautiful scent.

Inside is a metal removable vessel for a small charcoal and one or two pieces of incense. Once the charcoal is lit, small sparks flutter. Do not worry, this is indicative of the charcoal lighting. Replace the lid of the burner, and soon the smoldering charcoal will have released the aromatic oils from the incense. Walk through the house with the burner in your right hand and enter each room making the sign of the cross into the air with the burner. The house soon fills with the wonderful scent of burning frankincense or rose incense and provides a calming spiritual blessing for the home and its residents.

Entertaining

The Greek Hostess

The welcoming of guests into a Greek home is done with deep affection and warmth. The hosts are always eager to please their guests to ensure that their visit is both enjoyable and memorable. Usually there is a lot of lively conversation, storytelling, reminiscing, laughter, along with a touch of philosophy – and of course passions rise when politics is discussed.

Most Greek homes have a decorative bowl in which they keep chocolates, lollies, nougat or other sweets. Sweets are on hand, ready for serving to visitors and for family members to sneak a few too.

I have fond memories of visiting the David Jones food hall with my mother, and helping her select a lovely array of loose, colourful, foil-wrapped chocolates. We would take one of the cane baskets provided, and make our choices. The basket would be weighed, and sweets placed in the distinctive black and white houndstooth DJ's paper bags. At home, they would be placed in the crystal-footed serving bowl especially used for serving sweets.

It is usual for a hostess to prepare small bowls of dried sultanas, figs and dates, together with almonds, cashews, pistachios, dried chickpeas and sunflower seeds. These are placed onto the table of the room where visitors are received, and are offered to guests upon arrival.

Usually my parents would go to the local Greek emporium to buy xerous korpous (dried nuts) in bigger quantities, and my mother always stored them in large, airtight glass jars. That made it easier to see them, more convenient to serve and most importantly meant she knew when to replenish the supply.

Ouzo, cognac or other liqueur is offered with these nibbles followed by a Greek coffee served with the customary glass of water, and perhaps a spoon sweet, kourabiedes or melamakarona, or any other homemade treat.

Kerasma

Kerasma is the act of offering and serving food and drinks to visitors. Because Greeks are very house proud and inclusive by nature, and because much of their food is either home-grown or handmade, the offering of Kerasma is an act of pride, love and friendship. Greeks by nature love to entertain and share, and will do so in the most inviting way possible. Kerasma is a special gift of the naturally warm-hearted Greeks.

Upon entering a home the first questioned asked is, "Ti na se keraso?" ("What may I offer you?"). Regardless of how you respond, it's best to expect that you will indeed be offered whatever is available.

The Greek term for 'good appetite' is Kali Orexi, which is a wish for guests to literally have a good appetite and 'enjoy their meal'.

Philoxenia

Philoxenia can be described as the generous act of hospitality and kindness shown to a guest, a foreigner or stranger in one's own home. It is an act of thoughtfulness, caring and generosity that encompasses the unique Greek meaning of hospitality. The literal translation of philoxenia is 'befriending a stranger'. Philo is 'friend' and Xeno is 'stranger'.

Immediately upon arrival guests are offered a glass of water, and asked if they would like a coffee or something to eat. Sharing is also an important part of the Greek culture.

Our parents taught us that where there is love, there is room for an unexpected guest to dine at our table. This means that each person is served a smaller portion, to allow everyone to partake of the food. As children, we were never allowed to complain or show disappointment in our share being divided up to include a visitor.

Those employed at the home are cared for like one's own. Morning and afternoon coffee and biscuits are served, and in many homes lunch is also on menu. Outside of Greece, this generosity surprises most people who have not encountered the Greek act of Philoxenia.

φιλοσοφια

Philosophy

"Nobody can say a word against Greek: it stamps a man at once as an educated gentleman."

George Bernard Shaw

Ouzo and Meze

Drinking ouzo is a favourite pastime of Greeks both in Greece and abroad. It is the national drink and locals and tourists can be seen leisurely sipping the clear-coloured, aniseed-flavoured aperitif, either neat or over ice, as they sit at beachside tavernas or kafenion. Anyone who has travelled to Greece knows how cultured and civilized this pleasure can be. Taking ouzo and meze is conducive to the unique climate of Greece. Greeks love it. Tourists love it. Put simply… it's splendid!

More satisfying mezedes can be offered too. Favourite mezedes include; mouth-watering taramasalata (caviar dip); dolmades (rice wrapped in vine leaves); fresh calamari or whitebait that has been lightly floured, cooked in olive oil and drizzled with lemon juice; pickled or chargrilled octopus, and prawn saganaki (prawns in rich tomato salsa).

Traditionally, small portions of meze consisting of a few olives, a piece of cheese, and some cucumber and tomato are served with ouzo and a small carafe of water. My husband, George, and his father continue the tradition of ouzo and meze, and they both always look forward to catching up!

Ouzo is traditionally served in small, narrow glass tumblers that are short or mid-sized, and usually a little wider at the top. Water can be added to the ouzo, which turns the clear spirit a milky white colour, and some prefer to drink it on the rocks. However you take your ouzo, it has a distinctive aniseed taste and is a perfect way to start a meal. Stin iyeia mas! (Cheers! or To our health!)

Ouzo and mezedes are a lovely way for family and friends to meet up casually and enjoy one another's company. Mezedes are made for sharing with people that you love to be with and people you care for. There is a certain intimacy to partaking in mezedes since the only way to enjoy them is for the plates to be placed at the centre of the table for all to partake.

Greek Coffee

Most Greeks start the day with a cup of Greek coffee. This pulverized coffee is prepared in a briki, a small pot that is wider at the bottom and narrower at the top. It has a lip to make pouring easy and a long handle, which is needed for preparing the coffee over a stovetop to ensure that fingers don't get burnt. There are several sizes of brikia available, from a one-cup to an eight-cup pot. For larger quantities of coffee usually an electric briki is used.

Hosts ask whether their guests prefer their coffee to be pikro (bitter), metrio (medium) or glyko (sweet).

Usually a medium coffee consists of one heaped teaspoon of coffee and one level teaspoon of sugar, although some coffee drinkers may prefer it a little more bitter or a little sweeter. On occasion, Mum would spice up her Greek coffee with the addition of an aromatic clove bud, adding just a little more sweetness and spice.

How to make Greek Coffee

To prepare Greek coffee you will need an appropriate sized Briki and a long handled teaspoon. Put a heaped teaspoon of coffee per person into the briki.

Then, using a demitasse coffee cup, add the required number of cups of water to the briki, filled to just shy of the top of the cup, followed by the desired amount of sugar.

Take the briki to the stovetop and using a long handled teaspoon, begin to stir the pot until the sugar is dissolved.

Allow the coffee to rise to the top of the briki. A wonderful creamy froth will appear. This is called kaimaki (pronounced kay-maki) and you must act quickly so as to not lose this creamy froth. It's what distinguishes a well-made Greek coffee from the alternative.

Immediately take the briki off the heat and proceed to pour a small amount of froth into the cups. This allows the even distribution of the kaimaiki.

Continue to top up the cups with the remainder of the coffee. Serve immediately with a glass of cold water.

In traditional Greek homes, it is very likely that the hostess will offer spoon sweets when guests come to visit and this is especially the case if there are no home baked biscuits or cakes on offer, or indeed if visiting during Lent.

Using an abundance of seasonal fruits, spoon sweets are made for use throughout the year by combining the fruit with sugar and gently boiling until the fruit is coated in a rich, thick syrup. Rose Geranium leaves can be added to make the spoon sweets even more fragrant, or blanched slivered almonds that have been toasted add a lovely texture.

Spoon sweets are made from sultana grapes, cumquats, watermelon peel, figs, quince, citrus peels, cherries and walnuts, just to name a few. A heaped teaspoon of the preserve is placed onto a delicate plate and is served with a glass of chilled water and a Greek coffee.

Sultana Grapes
Spoon Sweet

My mother would make this delicious spoon sweet using white sultana grapes harvested from our grape vine. The aroma of clove buds was divine and the texture provided by the toasted blanched almonds perfectly complemented the sweetness of the grapes and syrup. We loved this special treat and mum proudly served her delicious conserve on the most beautiful hand painted porcelain plates with decorative spoons and of course the customary Greek coffee and a glass of chilled water.

Ingredients

1 kilogram small ripe sultana grapes

3 cups sugar

1/4 cup water

1 teaspoon lemon juice

3-4 whole clove buds

1/2 cup slivered or whole almonds, blanched and toasted

Method

Remove the grapes from the stems and wash well.

In a heavy based saucepan add the sugar, water, grapes and spices, and bring to the boil.

Reduce heat and simmer for 30-45 minutes until a syrup forms and the grapes are a lovely golden brown colour.

Add the lemon juice and simmer for another 5-10 minutes.

Remove the pan for the heat and stir in the slivered almonds.

Allow the mixture to cool and then pour into sterilised jars and seal.

Cumquat Spoon Sweet

The island of Corfu is well known and famous for cumquats. The islanders prepare delicious spoon sweets and liqueurs that are served both in the home and are available to purchase. I have a magnificent specimen of a very old cumquat tree in my garden and from time to time I prepare spoon sweets for use throughout the year. Because cumquats are naturally bitter, hot water is poured over the fruit to help remove some of the bitterness. Cumquat spoon sweets can be served with Greek coffee, with ice cream, yoghurt or used as a glaze on other cakes and dessert.

Ingredients

300 grams fresh cumquats

1 3/4 cups sugar

1 3/4 cups water

Method

Put the kettle on to boil.

Meanwhile take the cumquat fruit and remove any stems or leaves.

Wash the fruit well and then place them into a bowl.

Pour the boiled water over the fruits and leave until the water returns to room temperature.

Strain the cumquats in a colander.

In a heavy based saucepan add the sugar, water and cumquat fruit and bring to the boil.

Reduce heat and simmer for 30 to 45 minutes or until the syrup is thickened and set.

Allow the mixture to cool and then pour into sterilised jars and seal.

Spoon Sweet

Quinces also known as Kydonia in Greek resemble a large, furry, golden apple with firm, stringy flesh, and a delightful perfume. These bold fruits are harvested in late Autumn. The tart flavour of the quince makes it unappealing to eat raw, however when prepared as a spoon sweet this humble fruit is transformed into a delightful sweet treat that turns a beautiful hue of soft ruby red. When preparing quince it is important to work quickly and to place the sliced pieces into a bowl of water whilst cutting up the fruit as this helps to prevent discolouration. The spoon sweet can be fragranced with cinnamon, clove buds, vanilla or aromatic geranium leaves. Toasted blanched whole almonds or slivers, adds a lovely texture.

Ingredients

1 kg quince

3 1/2 cups sugar

3 1/2 cups water

1 cinnamon stick or 6 clove buds

2 tablespoons lemon juice

Method

Wash quinces, remove the core and cut into thin slices.

Place into a heavy based saucepan and combine with water, sugar and cinnamon or clove buds. Bring to the boil, and reduce heat to low and continue cooking until the fruit is soft and the syrup has thickened, but not too much. Add the lemon juice, stir and remove from heat. Allow to cool and then pour into sterilised jars and seal.

There are many childhood memories of taking a long-handled teaspoon, scooping out vanilla fondant, and then immersing it in a glass of iced water. Typically served in summer, this sweet fondant has a hint of vanilla and is quite refreshing, even if it is a little indulgent. The fondant is eaten in small bits, much like a lollipop, leaving the water with the subtle hint of vanilla. It's not a treat for every day, but is enjoyed a few times a year when the weather is hot.

Kitchen and Garden

Seasonal Gardening

Each spring my father plants a vast quantity of tomato bushes along with zucchini, cucumbers, eggplants and wild greens. He nurtures his garden lovingly and harvests his produce with pride. We all receive a fair share of his unrivalled gardening efforts, proudly handed to us when we visit. My husband and I are especially fortunate as both our dads are expert gardeners and spoil us with their magnificent offerings.

Each summer, my parents prepared homemade tomato salsa from the many kilos of tomatoes harvested from their garden. The tomatoes are roughly cut, sprinkled with salt and allowed to drain prior to being pureed through a tomato press to separate the juice from the tomato skins and seeds. This process is repeated several times to ensure that the rich thick tomato paste, known as pasta, is pressed from the skins and captured to give the homemade salsa that extra richness. The thick red juice is then funnelled into large brown beer bottles, sealed and boiled, and stored for future use.

Every couple of years in the autumn, grapes are ordered from a favourite vineyard and delivery is anticipated with excitement. Many years back the old method of making wine was adopted, with the fruit placed into a cast iron bathtub and all of us taking turns to tread the fruit. Over the last few decades, Dad has adopted the more modern method of passing the grapes through a press and then pouring the juice into a barrel to ferment for forty days. The result is a table wine the colour of cognac, free of chemical additives, and one that Dad especially enjoys sharing with us all at meal times.

Our family uses surplus grape juice in two different ways. Firstly, some is prepared into Moustalevria (grape must pudding) using fresh grape juice thickened with semolina and topped with toasted sesame seeds, cinnamon and coarsely chopped walnuts. The remainder of the grape juice is poured into a large, heavy-based pot and boiled until it has reduced to become a rich, thick, and dark syrup called Petimezi. This is used throughout the year to serve on loukoumathes (honey puffs), tiganites (pancakes) and added to moustokouloura (grape must biscuits) that Mum expertly baked.

In winter the garden is abundant with wild greens for boiling. Horta, as they are called, are washed, boiled, then drained in a colander, placed into a serving dish, sprinkled with a little salt, and dressed using olive oil and white vinegar or lemon juice. These wild greens are a perfect accompaniment to seafood, grilled meat and poultry, and are very nutritious too.

φιλοσοφια

Philosophy

"Let food be your medicine and medicine be your food."

Hippocrates

The Essential Ingredients

The essence of Greek cuisine is simple; good quality, fresh ingredients, lovingly prepared to give the best rustic, authentic and flavoursome food.

In many Greek homes, ingredients are harvested from gardens that are tenderly and expertly cared for. An abundance of tomatoes, peppers, aubergine and cucumbers are grown in the summer, and a variety of lettuces, leeks and wild greens are grown in the winter.

Herb gardens are an important inclusion in any Greek garden. It allows cooks to infuse their dishes with freshly picked ingredients that provide optimal flavours. It is a truly wonderful experience to go out onto the balcony or herb patch and collect the necessary ingredients to add flavour and zest to lovingly prepared homemade meals.

Essential ingredients include olive oil, lemon, rigani, tomato, dill, parsley, mint, pulses, feta and other cheeses, yoghurt, olives, a range of seafood, poultry and meat, and many spices, including cloves, cinnamon, nutmeg, black and white pepper, cumin, mahlepi and pimento, to name a few.

Greek cooking varies from region to region as recipes have evolved using the local produce that grows in each region. It is, however, always extremely healthy and delicious. A balance of ingredients is essential so that the meal is colourful, appetizing and healthy. Most dishes that include meat or poultry can be made equally delicious in a vegetarian version of that recipe. This is essential for the many days of fasting that occur throughout the Orthodox calendar.

Usually Greeks enjoy fresh seasonal fruit, nuts or yoghurt after a meal. Most recipes call for nuts, honey, citrus and cinnamon, and sweets are made for special occasions.

Greek cooks also expertly preserve fruits and vegetables to be used throughout the year. This can range from making tomato paste, pickled vegetables and olives (salt-dried and prepared in brine), through to the preserving of citrus fruit peels for use as a spoon sweet.

μαλακό
MIN

Natural Remedies

Greeks love using the ingredients from nature's kitchen. Many Greek gardens include medicinal plants such as mint, chamomile and sage, and no true Greek home would be without these essentials.

Sage

Sage is a pleasant-tasting medicinal tea used for treating inflammation of the mouth and throat. It is also helpful in cooling a fever and in cleansing the body.

Put a few dried sage leaves into a pot and add freshly boiled water to make the tea. Allow the leaves to infuse for 2-5 minutes. Serve with a slice of lemon and, if desired, sweeten with sugar or honey.

Camomile flowers are usually gathered from the home gardens or from fields where it grows wildly. The camomile is then air-dried and stored in glass jars.

To make chamomile tea, water is brought to the boil on the stovetop and ½ teaspoon of dried camomile is added and stirred until the tea is brewed. This tea requires straining through a fine tealeaf sieve or through a piece of clean linen.

Usually served with sugar or honey, this tea is an excellent remedy for aches and pains as it relaxes the body. Camomile tea is also very helpful in treating menstrual cramps.

Mint

Mint grows freely in the garden or in pots on a balcony or terrace. In Greek cuisine, both dried and fresh leaves are used as an herb in cooking.

Dried mint leaves are used to make a refreshing tea and as an excellent tonic to aid digestion. To make mint tea, simply bring a pot of water to the boil on the stovetop, add a few dried mint leaves and allow to brew. The tea is naturally sweet, however it may be sweetened to taste using sugar or honey.

Greek Mountain Tea

Greek mountain tea is made from the dried flowers of ironwort, which is usually found on rocky slopes in the Greek mountains.

Mountain tea is a popular drink and is mostly used for helping relieve symptoms of colds, indigestion, aches and pains. It can also be used to soothe mild nervousness or anxiety.

To enjoy this lovely tea, put a few dried ironwort flowers into a pot and add freshly boiled water. Allow to infuse for 5 minutes. Serve with a slice of lemon and honey, if desired.

Lemon Verbena

Louisa, also known as Lemon Verbena is a shrub with long pointy leaves that feels a little rough to touch. When gently bruised between the fingers, this delightful garden plant releases a wonderfully delicious scent of lemon. The leaves can be harvested, dried and used to make a beneficial herbal tea. Louisa helps aid digestion, provides relief from anxiety, is used as a sedative to help with relaxation, and is believed to induce peaceful sleep.

Place a few dried leaves into a teapot and add freshly boiled water. Allow to infuse for 10 minutes. Serve with honey if desired.

Dill

Anitho

Dill has a slightly aniseed flavour and is said to stimulate the appetite and aid digestion. It is frequently added to lettuce salads, especially a cos lettuce salad that is dressed with a sprinkling of salt, olive oil and lemon juice. Dill is used to flavor dolmades (rice-stuffed vine leaves) and is an essential ingredient in many other dishes, especially those containing artichokes, broad beans or peas. Its delicate leaves are often used as a garnish.

Vasilikos

Basil is used as an ornament in the garden or for religious purposes. It is believed to have grown where Helen and Constantine found the Holy Cross, making it a much-revered plant not usually included in traditional Greek recipes.

Greek homes often have pots of trimmed basil at either side of the front or back door, on the balcony or terrace, as it is a blessed plant that will bring health and a spiritual blessing. It is usual for men to pick a little sprig of basil and place it over one of their ears as it is thought to provide clarity of mind and peacefulness.

Για χάρη του βασιλικού ποτίζεται κι η γλάστρα

For the sake of the Basil plant, the pot is watered also

Marantho

This anise-flavoured herb is very similar to dill with its feathery, fern-like, dark green leaves. It has a distinct licorice flavour and is a key ingredient in koukia (broad bean stew), fricassee dishes, kolokithokeftethes (zuchini croquets) and meat or vegetable ragouts. Fennel grows easily in a Mediterranean climate with very little attention needed for it to be grown in home gardens. The leaves can also be added to salads, tzatziki, or used as a garnish.

Madzourana

This herb is very similar to oregano, however is a little sweeter in flavour. It can be added to meat and poultry dishes and in some parts of Greece the leaves are hand-picked from the stems and sprinkled onto Greek salad.

Rigani

Known as Greek oregano, Rigani is an essential ingredient in traditional Greek cuisine. The leaves are harvested, dried and stored in jars for use throughout the year. A pinchful is rubbed between the palms and sprinkled over sun-ripened tomatoes, onto a Horiatiki Salata (Greek Salad), over feta cheese, added to a meatball mixture, and rubbed over lamb before roasting. The sweet and spicy aroma adds that wonderful flavour typical of many Greek savoury dishes.

Parsley

Maindano

Traditionally in Greek cuisine the flat-leaf parsley is preferred over the curly-leaf variety. Chopped roughly, or finely, it is used in many dishes including salad, stews, poultry, meat and seafood. The leaves are also used as a garnish. Most traditional Greek gardens would have this much-used herb growing freely.

Rosemary

Dendrolivano

The sweet-smelling, needle-like leaves of rosemary, whether used dried or fresh, enhance the flavour of roasted meats, and especially lamb. Rosemary is a very easy herb to grow as it is quite drought tolerant, and during the summer months it produces tiny blue blossoms that make it an ideal garden specimen too.

Arbaroriza

These sweetly-scented leaves are used sparingly to enhance spoon sweets and jams by providing a beautifully delicate flavour. The leaves are also used to decorate the Red-Dyed Easter Eggs.

Aniseed

Likaniso

This aromatic spice is harvested from the anise seed that is then dried and ground ready to be added to both sweet and savoury dishes. Anise has a very similar taste to that of licorice and is used as the key ingredient in Greek Ouzo, giving it that distinctive taste and aroma. Small amounts of the sweet-smelling and highly aromatic ground anise seeds are also added to rusks and bread.

Bay Leaves

Dafni

Bay leaves have a distinctive flavour and are used to flavour soups and stews as well as added to the brine of pickled vegetables.

These aromatic leaves are especially used in Lentil soup (fakes), and are the key fragrant ingredient to a well-known Greek slow cooked meat dish known as stifado that is made with either beef, game or poultry and pearl onions studded with clove buds.

Cinnamon

Kanela

The beautifully aromatic quills of cinnamon are used in Greek cooking for both sweet and savoury dishes. Added to kapama (chicken cooked in tomato salsa), cinnamon makes this dish very distinctive and flavoursome. The quills are also used in Greek syrup cakes, and dried cinnamon is added to semolina dishes or sprinkled on top of rizogalo (rice pudding).

Clove Buds

Garifalo

Aromatic dried clove buds are added to both savoury and sweet dishes, and the flavor adds warmth to any recipe. Cloves enhance the sweetness and spiciness of everything from slow-cooked meat stews to syrups for cakes. When cooking stifado, cloves are used to stud the whole pearl onions to make the dish not only aromatic, but also pleasing to the eye.

Nutmeg

Moshokarydo

Nutmeg is available as a ground powder or as a whole nut. It is used sparingly as it has a strong taste and is highly aromatic. It is used to infuse the béchamel sauce for pastitsio and moussaka and is added when baking sweets or is sprinkled over risogalo (rice pudding). A grater will be required if using the whole nut.

Sesame Seeds

Sousami

These tiny seeds are used to sprinkle over the traditional Greek rusks, koulourakia (biscuits), breads, and are one of the main ingredients in Pastelli (sesame and honey sweets). Sesame seeds are also dry roasted and ground to a paste for adding to kolliva.

Cumin

Kymino

Cumin is native to the Mediterranean, and has been used as a seasoning in Greek food since ancient times. This aromatic spice is known to be high in iron as well as being beneficial to digestion. When added to cooking, cumin infuses food with a deliciously, slightly nutty, and warming flavour. My mother-in-law added a little ground cumin to her famous meatballs, and at times, I like to add a pinch to baked eggplant.

φιλοσοφια

Philosophy

"The name Greek is no longer a mark of a race, but of an outlook, and is accorded to those who share our culture rather than our blood."

Isocrates, Athenian orator, 380 BC

This recipe is simple and delicious and is a popular dish from the Ionian Islands. It is especially prepared in Zakynthos, the island where my grandfather was born.

My mother made Riganada for our family when tomatoes were plentiful and picked fresh from the garden. The oregano used was also harvested from the garden, and air-dried ready to be hand-rubbed over the ripe, juicy tomatoes.

This treat was prepared for my sister and me to keep us still whilst mum styled our hair. Dressed in our baby-doll pyjamas after bathtime, Mum would sit us on a stool each holding a plate of this delicious snack.

Ingredients

A ripe tomato (cut in half, and gently squeezed of excess juice and seeds)

Fresh bread

A sprinkling of hand-rubbed rigani

Salt for seasoning

Method

Using the most ripe, home-grown tomatoes and fresh bread, simply cut a generous slice of bread, drizzle with the best olive oil, and take the cut tomato to squeeze the pulp onto the bread. Sprinkle with hand-rubbed rigani (oregano) and salt.

For as far back as I can remember, my mother would spend hours preparing handmade and hand-cut pasta squares called hilopites.

Hilopites are quite rustic looking, and because they are hand-cut it seems that no two pieces are alike. Essential to making this pasta are free-range fresh eggs. Naturally our eggs were collected from our very own chicken coop.

To make hilopites, flour is placed into a shallow dish or directly onto a wooden board. My mother made a well in the centre of the flour and, with her expert skills, would crack the eggs using only one hand! After adding them one by one to the flour, Mum would proceed to add milk and semolina to the mix. The ingredients were kneaded well to form a malleable dough that was then rolled out quite thinly and allowed to dry for a short period of time. Using a sharp knife, my mother would slice the pasta into strips, then the strips into squares, then place them on clean white linen tablecloths for air-drying. This usually would take 3-5 days depending on the weather and the season.

When the hilopites were all dry Mum would wrap the cloth into a bundle, tie with string and hang for a few weeks to make sure that they were completely dried. The hilopities would then be stored in clear glass jars, and naturally we would all get our fair share of these special homemade pasta squares!

Home-made egg pasta

Ingredients

1 cup milk

1 tsp salt

1/4 cup semolina

3 cups plain flour

3 eggs

Method

Place the flour and semolina in a bowl or on a work surface. Create a well in the middle of the dry ingredients.

Add the eggs, a little of the milk, and using a fork begin to mix.

Continue to add the milk, and using your hand gather the flour in a little at a time to form a soft dough.

More flour or milk may be required to achieve a soft malleable dough.

Knead for approximately 5 minutes or until the dough is smooth. Cover with a clean tea towel and set aside for 20 minutes.

Divide the dough into manageable pieces.

Dust a clean surface with flour and using a rolling pin roll out the dough just slightly, and set aside to rest.

Continue to roll out all the manageable pieces until your have several pieces of rolled out dough that is resting.

Take the rested rolled-out dough and continue to roll each one out as thin as possible.

Lay these out onto a clean tablecloth for approximately an hour to slightly air dry as this will make it more manageable for cutting.

Using a sharp knife cut into long thin strips approximately 1/2 inch wide. Proceed to then cut the strips into small squares.

Repeat the cutting with the remaining dough.

Spread the hilopites on a clean tablecloth. Allow to dry in a cool and well ventilated spot for a few days. When completely dry store the Hilopites in clean and sterilized jars.

Trahana

Sweet

Trahana is a coarse grain-like pasta made with flour and yoghurt. The addition of the yoghurt imparts a sour flavour to this homemade pasta. Mum would lay out clean white linen cloths and lay the trahana on top to air-dry. Later the trahana would be stored in glass jars and added to vegetarian tomato soup that was made with either fresh tomatoes harvested from the garden or homemade tomato salsa, olive oil, salt and pepper.

Ingredients

1 litre of milk

1 tablespoon salt

750 grams flour

750 grams coarse semolina

Method

Boil the milk, reduce heat, add salt and stir well.

Very slowly add the wheat flour and semolina, stirring constantly with a wooden spoon, until thick.

Remove from the heat and cover with a clean cotton tea towel.

Allow the mixture to cool.

Pinch off small pieces of the dough and place them on a clean cotton tablecloth and then leave to dry in a dark and airy spot.

When dried, using your hands crumb the pieces into coarse granules.

Return the granules to a clean tablecloth and place into a cool, well-ventilated place for 4-5 days, or until completely dry. Store in clean sterilized jars.

Sour

Ingredients

1 litre of milk

3/4 cup natural yoghurt

1 tablespoon salt

750 grams flour

750 grams coarse semolina

Method

Place the milk in a glass bowl.

Add the yogurt and mix well with a wooden spoon.

Cover with a clean tea towel and then place a blanket on top to keep the mixture warm.

Let stand in a warm place for approximately about half a day.

Stir from time to time using a wooden spoon.

Slowly add the semolina and flour and mix until a thick dough forms.

Pinch off small pieces and place them on a clean cotton tablecloth and then dry in a dark and airy spot.

When dried, using your hands crumb the pieces into coarse granules.

Return the granules to a clean tablecloth and place into a cool and well-ventilated place for 4-5 days, or until completely dry. Store in clean sterilized jars.

Pigeon Ragout

Mum would prepare our home-raised pigeons into a delicious slow-cooked ragout with chopped onion, olive oil, homemade red wine, salt, pepper and rigani. This dish was traditionally served at our Easter supper. At other times Mum would add tomato salsa to this dish and serve it with the homemade hilopites. It was an absolutely delicious and delightful meal!

Ingredients

4 pigeons, cleaned and washed

1/2 cup of olive oil

1 medium onion, finely chopped

1/3rd cup red wine

3 tablespoons tomato paste

1 cup water

5 clove buds

salt and pepper to taste

1/2 cup of long grain rice, rinsed or 1/2 cup home made hilopites

Method

Cut the birds into quarters and dry using absorbent paper.

Heat the olive oil in a heavy based saucepan.

Brown the pigeons on all sides.

Remove and set aside.

Saute the onion in the pan until soft.

Return the birds to the pan and pour over the red wine.

Stir, and then add the clove buds, tomato paste, water, salt and pepper.

Cook gently and if required add extra hot water from the kettle.

Continue to simmer until tender.

When there are approximately 2 cups of liquid in the saucepan, increase the heat to bring to the boil and a gently add the rice or hilopites.

Stir, cover, reduce heat and simmer until the rice is cooked.

ΨΥΧΡΗΣ ΕΚΘΛΙΨΗΣ
ΑΡΓΟΛΙΣ
ΤΟ ΧΡΥΣΟ ΛΑΔΙ
ΦΑΚΛΑΡΗ Α.Ε.
4 ΛΙΤΡΑ
Αργολίς

KALAMATA
SELECTED BLACK OLIVES
NATURAL
PASTEURIZED
SUPER LUX
PACKERS & SHIPPERS
SIFONIOS
Kolympari
S.A.
Mihelakis Family
Native Olivenöl Extra Aus Kreta*
500 ml. (16.5 fl. oz.) e
Οικογένειας Μιχελάκη
ΚΟΛΥΜΒΑΡΙ
Εξαιρετικό Παρθένο Ελαιόλαδο*
Mihelakis Family
KOLYMVARI
Natives Olivenöl Extra*
Huile d'Olive Extra Vierge*
500 ml. (16.9 fl. oz.) e
ΕΛΑΙΑΙ
ΚΑΛΑΜΩΝ ΕΚΛΕΚΤΑΙ
ΦΥΣΙΚΑΙ
ΠΑΣΤΕΡΙΩΜΕΝΑΙ
SUPER LUX
ΣΙΦΩΝΙΟΣ
KALAMATA
SELECTED OLIVES
ΕΛΑΙΑΙ
ΕΚΛΕΚΤΑΙ ΕΛΛΑΔΟΣ
ΜΑΥΡΑΙ
ΦΥΣΙΚΑΙ
ΠΑΣΤΕΡΙΩΜΕΝΑΙ
SUPER LUX
ΣΙΦΩΝΙΟΣ
500 gr

Olive oil is a vital ingredient in the Mediterranean diet, and is used liberally in cooking and in dressing vegetables and salads. The olive tree grows well in Mediterranean and similar climates, and has been used by the Greeks for thousands of years. The harvesting of olives takes place in mid-Autumn, and in home gardens the olives are hand-picked and salt-cured or prepared in brine.

In Ancient Olympia, athletes rubbed olive oil over their bodies, and the victors were crowned with olive wreaths. In modern times, a Greek table would not be complete without a small bowl of olives to enjoy with a fresh piece of bread as an appetizer before a meal, or a bottle of extra virgin olive oil for adding to meals - especially those prepared with beans and pulses.

Olive oil has many uses. It has medicinal application, and is used as a massage oil, in cooking, to light the kandili (memorial candle), and for other religious purposes, including being rubbed over the bodies of babies before they are immersed in the baptismal font. Homer called it 'liquid gold'.

Dried Black Olives

Greek Style

Salted, dried olives can be prepared in one of two ways. You can either use a bucket pricked with holes, or a clean pillow slip to contain the olives.

Fill the pillow slip with olives, and tie securely before hanging from an elevated position. Be sure to place a vessel beneath the bucket or the pillow slip to capture the juices. Both options allow the juices of the salted olives to drain easily.

Ingredients

Kalamata olives

Coarse salt,1kg salt per 10 kg olives

Large bucket pricked with holes

Method

Hand-pick very ripe and unblemished olives.

Wash the olives and place them into a bucket.

Determine the quantity of salt required, and add to the olives.

Shake to mix the salt through the olives.

Continue to turn the olives each day for 15 days.

It is recommended to check the taste of the cured olives for bitterness, by tasting an olive that has been rinsed to remove the salt.

When the olives have been cured to your liking, shake off the excess salt and gently coat with a good quality olive oil and store in large sterilized air-tight containers.

Olives in Brine

Greek Style

Ingredients

Olives

Water

Coarse Salt

Method

Place the olives in a bucket and cover with water.

To keep the olives immersed weigh them down with an appropriate sized dinner plate, facing upwards, that will fit comfortably inside the bucket.

Change the water daily for 10 days.

On the last day, pour off the water and measure 2/3 of that quantity to determine the amount of brine required.

To make the brine, measure the equivalent of 2/3 of fresh water and bring to the boil.

Using a ratio of 1 cup of coarse salt to 10 cups of water, add the required amount of salt and dissolve in the water. Allow to cool completely.

Place the olives in clean jars or in one large container.

Add 1/3 quantity of white wine vinegar and 2/3 quantity of brine. Ensure that all the olives are immersed.

Pour approximately 1cm of olive oil into the jar to seal and prevent air from affecting the fruit.

Store the jars in a dark, cool position or in a cupboard.

Allow to cure for at least 6 weeks, before eating.

φιλοσοφια

Philosophy

"All virtue is summed up in dealing justly."

Aristotle

Greeks enjoy drinking table wine with their meals. Retsina is the most popular white wine and is enjoyed especially with more substantial mezedes and at meal times. Retsina has a distinct resin taste as a result of the pine wood placed into the barrel at the time of fermentation. Wine is only consumed with food and is not generally consumed between meals.

Retsina is exclusively made in Greece, and is a perfect accompaniment to the flavours of lemon, oregano, olive oil and tomato ingredients that are used in traditional Greek cooking.

In Greek tavernas and homes you will see that retsina is served in small tumblers and not in stemmed wine glasses. This table wine is unassuming and requires the rim of the glass to be open and not curved inwards, as would be the case for stemmed wine glasses.

It is thought that the resin flavour of retsina goes back to ancient times when the clay amphorae were lined with pine resin to seal the pots from air and spoilage during transportation.

Greece also produces other wines such as the dry, bold, rich red wines that are ideal for serving with meat dishes and casseroles during the winter, rose, and also sweet dessert wines like Mavrodaphne.

Greeks have enjoyed wine for thousands of years and it has been an important part of Greek heritage and culture, and in small quantities it is believed to provide many health benefits.

ΣΥΛΛΟΓΟΣ ΗΛΕΙΩΝ Ν.Α.
Η ΟΛΥΜΠΙΑΚΗ ΦΛΟΓΑ
Τιμητικό Δίπλωμα
MALAMATINA
μιά ζωή
DRY WHITE WINE
RETSINA
TRADITIONAL APPELLATION
e 2L
TABLE WINE
11% ALC/VOL
PRODUCED AND BOTTLED BY E. MALAMATINA AND SON S.A
THESSALONIKI - GREECE
PRODUCT OF GREECE
PRESERVATIVE (220) ADDED
ΑΔ. ΕΜΦ. 1/88 Γ.Χ.Κ. ΘΕΣ ΝΙΚΗΣ
33 ADAM STREET HINDMARSH
ΚΑΤΑΚΟΛΟ
OUZO
δίμηνο
Μυτιλήνης
ΜΕ ΑΠΟΣΤΑΓΜΑ
RETSINA
STANDARD DRINKS
OUZO
δίμηνο
Μυτιλήνης
ΜΕ ΑΠΟΣΤΑΓΜΑ
RETSINA
TRADITIONAL APPELLATION
ΜΥΤΙΛΗΝΗΣ

PROTECTED DESIGNATION OF ORIGIN
APPELLATION D' ORIGINE PROTÉGÉE
MAVRODAPHNE
from
de
Patras
RED LIQUEUR WINE - VIN DE LIQUEUR ROUGE

Feta cheese is the most well known Greek cheese and is available in various textures; soft, semi-soft, or crumbly. It is perfect as a mezze, or crumbed and sprinkled over Saganaki (prawns baked in rich tomato salsa).

Feta literally translates to slice, and is usually served as such. It adorns an Horiatiki Salata (Greek Salad), and can be sprinkled with rubbed rigani and drizzled with extra virgin olive oil.

Myzithra cheese is piquant, salty, flavoursome, and it is traditionally grated finely and sprinkled over makaronada (macaroni pasta).

Kasseri is a pale yellow and medium-textured cheese that is ideal for mezze platters.

Kefalotyri cheese is a hard, salty, yellow cheese that can be grated and sprinkled over pasta, or lightly floured and fried in a little olive oil to make the delicious mezze of cheese saganaki, served with a lemon wedge.

Kefalograviera is very similar to a Gruyere, and can be used as a table cheese, for mezze or for grating over pasta and other dishes.

Honey

Honey is an essential ingredient in the preparation of Greek sweets. It is also used for medicinal purposes, and added to tea as a sweetener. Honey comes in a variety of flavours, dependent on the nectar from which it has been sourced. There can be lemon, orange, eucalypt and pine-flavoured honey in either dark, light or medium colour and texture.

Mastic

Mastic or Mastiha is a plant resin that is obtained from the mastic tree. It is famously sourced from the Greek Island of Chios that has the reputation of supplying the best Mastic available. The dried resin is an opaque white colour, irregular in shape and is highly aromatic. Using a mortar and pestle the resin is ground with a little sugar for addition to Easter Tsoureki, which gives it that distinctive flavour.

Fanouropita is a traditional Greek cake prepared especially on the 26th of August, which is the eve of Saint Fanourios, or on the occasion of losing something, needing direction, wishing for good health, happiness and love. August 27th is the name day of Saint Fanourios, whose name comes from the Greek word fanero, which means 'to reveal'.

This aromatic cake is made with fresh orange juice, spices, walnuts and raisins and because it is a Lenten cake the recipe does not include eggs, milk or butter.

Over the years, it has become practice to prepare this cake when needing to reveal lost objects, restoring health, finding a job, seeking direction, or to reveal actions that should be taken. I remember my mother searching a sideboard cupboard in her dining room for something that she had misplaced, and had not yet found. She proceeded to ask Saint Fanourios to help her reveal the lost item!

Ingredients

3/4 cup sunflower oil

1 cup freshly squeezed orange juice

1/4 cup brandy or water

1 cup caster sugar

2 teaspoons ground cinnamon

1/2 teaspoon ground cloves

3 cups self raising flour

1/2 cup finely chopped walnuts

1 cup roughly chopped raisins

Method

Preheat oven to 180 degrees and line a round cake tin with baking paper.

Place the sunflower oil, orange juice, brandy, sugar, cinnamon, cloves and zest into a bowl and mix well with a whisk until the sugar dissolves slightly.

Gradually add the sifted flour, stir in the walnuts and raisins and mix well.

Pour the mixture into the baking tin and bake for approximately 45 minutes.

Allow the cake to cool and dust with icing sugar before serving.

Creamy Rice Pudding

This delicious and creamy Greek-style rice pudding is a favourite for an after-school snack, sometimes enjoyed as breakfast, definitely dished up in the afternoon and often enjoyed in the evening. Whatever the time, whatever the question, the answer is Rizogalo.

Ingredients

1 cup of water

1/2 cup short grain rice

4 cups milk

1 tablespoon butter

pinch of salt

1/4 cup sugar

1/2 teaspoon vanilla essence

ground nutmeg or cinnamon

Method

Place the water in a large pot, bring to the boil and add the short grain rice.

Cook gently for a few minutes whilst stirring.

Add the milk, butter and salt and gently bring to the boil.

Reduce the heat and stir occasionally until the rice is soft and the mixture creamy.

Add the sugar and vanilla and stir until dissolved.

Pour into individual serving bowls and dust with nutmeg or cinnamon.

Enjoy warm or chilled.

Grape Juice Pudding

This recipe is made once a year as a way to use up any extra grape juice from the fruit pressed in the winemaking process. At home we looked forward to this delicious treat that signalled the finale to the wine making process. My husband's mother spoils us each year with this delicious pudding that is infused with warm spices and topped with toasted sesame seeds and chopped walnuts. It is a lovely pudding that is best served chilled with a glass of iced water, or of course with a Greek coffee.

Ingredients

2 cups of fresh grape juice (from winemaking)

1/4 cup sugar

1/4 cup fine semolina

Pinch of ground cloves

1/4 teaspoon ground cinnamon

1/2 cup chopped walnuts

2 tablespoons sesame seeds toasted

Extra cinnamon

Method

Place the grape juice, sugar and semolina into a large pot and bring to the boil.

Stir constantly until the mixture begins to bubble and thicken.

Add the cloves and cinnamon and stir through gently. Continue cooking for a few more minutes.

Pour into one large serving bowl or individual bowls.

Sprinkle with walnuts, sesame seeds and cinnamon.

It is best chilled before serving.

Petimezi
Grape Syrup

Petimezi is made from the first press of grape juice sourced in the winemaking process. The wood ash helps clarify the grape juice of any unwanted grape seeds or grape skins, and the fine muslin cloth will further clarify the juice. When making petimezi it is essential to not leave the juice unattended when cooking. My mother made this syrupy grape juice each time we made wine, and took much care to ensure that a good quantity of petimizi was made to last throughout the year. This delightful syrup is poured over pancakes (tiganites), honey puffs (loukoumades), as an ingredient in Moustokouloura (Grape must biscuits), or used sparingly on toast. Mum would give us a teaspoon of petimezi as a treat and as a natural soother whenever we had a sore throat!

Ingredients

10 litres of fresh grape juice

3 tablespoons wood ash

Method

Pour the desired quantity of juice into a large heavy based pot together with a a few tablespoons of wood ash, and bring to the boil. Lower the heat and gently simmer uncovered for approximately 15 minutes whilst skimming off the froth that rises to the top.

Turn off the heat and allow to cool overnight, and to allow the sediment to sink to the bottom of the pot.

The next day, place a sieve that has been lined with fine muslin over another pot and carefully pour the juice into the sieve. The muslin cloth will capture the sediment, further clarifying the juice.

Take this pot to the stove and bring to the boil.

Reduce the heat to a gentle simmer and be sure to watch over the juice as it thickens into a deep red, brown syrup.

Be careful as Petemezi can easily boil over or burn, and quickly ruin if left unattended.

Petemezi is ready when the syrup coats the back of the spoon.

Allow to cool slightly and then using a funnel pour into sterilised bottles or jars and store in a dark, cool place.

Ravani tou Mourias

Baked Semolina Cake

A delightful and special recipe for Ravani tou Mourias, also known as Moriatikos Halvas. This is a delicious oven-baked semolina cake especially made in the area surrounding Pyrgos Ilias in the Peloponnese. My mother regularly baked this cake for our family as it was a favourite when we were growing up. The mixture would be pressed into a baking tray, cut into diamond shapes, and each piece was topped with a blanched almond before baking. Importantly because this recipe is measured in cups, the quantity can be amended simply by using smaller or larger cups. The best part of baking this cake is scraping the edges of the baking dish and as children we fought over who was going to get the best bit!

Ingredients

2/12 cups sugar

21/2 cups semolina

1 cup sunflower oil or light olive oil

31/2 cups hot water from the kettle

1 tsp pure vanilla essence (optional)

3/4 cup whole blanched almonds

Method

Preheat the oven to 180 degrees.

In a heavy based saucepan mix the sugar, semolina and oil.

Place over a medium heat and continue stirring with a wooden spoon.

Gradually add the water and vanilla essence, and stir constantly until the mixture thickens and comes away from the edge of the pot.

Grease a large baking tray with a little oil and dust lightly with flour to help prevent the mixture from sticking.

Place the mixture into the pan and smooth down with the back of a wooden spoon or spatula.

Cut into diamond shapes appropriate for individual serves and decorate each piece with a whole blanched almond.

Bake in a moderate oven for approximately 1 hour until golden brown.
Allow to cool in the baking tray before removing to a serving platter.

Galatopita

Baked Milk Pudding

This was one of our favourite dishes to come home to. The aroma of milk and vanilla-baked pudding was mouthwatering. My mother's recipe is especially delicious and the nicest part is scraping the edges out of the baking dish and eating them with a spoon. Galatopita is also enjoyable when served chilled.

Ingredients

1 litre of milk

1 cup water

1 cm slice of unsalted butter

1 teaspoon grated lemon rind

2 1/2 cups of fine semolina

1 1/2 cups of sugar

2 teaspoons vanilla essence

6 eggs

Method

Place the milk, water, unsalted butter, sugar and lemon zest into a large pot and warm until sugar has dissolved.

Mix in the semolina and constantly stir until the mixture begins to thicken.

Take off the heat and allow to cool a little.

Whisk up the eggs in a bowl and, working quickly, mix the eggs into the semolina mixture.

Add vanilla essence.

Place in a baking dish and bake for 30-40 minutes.

Home made yoghurt is easy to make and delicious to eat. It's best prepared in the late evening so that the yoghurt can set undisturbed overnight. For a thicker style yoghurt, place the previously prepared yoghurt into a clean linen towel. Using some kitchen string tie a knot and hang over a tap to allow the liquid to drain. The result is creamy yoghurt that can be eaten plain, or topped with honey and chopped nuts, served with fruit or mixed with drained grated cucumber to make tzatziki.

Ingredients

1/2 cup natural plain yoghurt

1 litre of milk

A large round cake tin or other vessel to hold the glasses

Method

Pour the milk into a saucepan and bring almost to the boil.

Turn off the heat and remove the saucepan to allow the milk to cool. This may take some 20-30 minutes.

When tepid (test using your pinky finger), take 1/2 cup of the tepid milk and mix well with the natural plain yogurt. Add this mixture to the remainder of the milk and stir well.

Put the kettle on to boil and in the meantime place approximately 6-8 glasses, depending on size, into the vessel.

Pour the yogurt mixture into the glasses.

Pour the boiled water into the vessel making sure that no water spills into the yoghurt filled glasses.

Cover with a clean tea towel and then place a clean folded blanket over the vessel to keep the mixture warm and to allow the yoghurt to set.

Let the mixture sit overnight, and in the morning you will have fresh Greek natural yoghurt.

OUZO
δίμηνο
OUZO
δίμηνο
ΚΑΤΑΚΟΛΟ

Greek Way of Life

Traditions

When a child loses their baby teeth

When a child loses their baby teeth, the tradition calls for the parent to take the tooth and throw it up on to the roof whilst reciting the following verse:

Κουρουνα παρε το δοντι μου και δως μου σιδερενιο, να ροκαναω τα μυγδαλα, να τρωω τα παξιμαδια.

This loosely translates to:

Crow take my tooth, and replace it with a silver one
So, that I can break up almonds, and eat rusks.

I remember as a child standing in the backyard beside my father as he recited this little verse whilst throwing my tooth up onto the roof, and then bending down and giving me a hug and a kiss. I always wondered if somehow I would ever see it again. My friends at school kept their lost teeth in little decorative boxes or a glass filled with water, for the tooth fairy to deliver some coins. On reflection, there are some similarities in what we wished for. In Greek culture, a silver tooth replaced the lost one, and my friends received silver coins for their lost teeth.

On the occasion of buying something new

Greeks love celebrating and bestowing good wishes and blessings at any opportunity.

It is customary when someone acquires a new piece of clothing, shoes or accessories to be bestowed with the words, “Me Yeia” (pronounced Me-ya), which literally translates to “with health”. This good wish is to bless the person to be fortunate enough to wear their new item, or items, with good health.

The blessing bestowed for the purchase of something bigger, for example a car or a new home is, “Kaloriziko” (pronounced ka-lo-rEE-ziko), which translates to “good luck”.

φιλοσοφια

Philosophy

"Love is all we have, the only way that each can help the other."

Euripides

The Greek Key

The Greek key is one of the most recognizable symbols associated with Greece. It is a geometric, decorative border in a meandering style that is used in various forms. It is seen on architectural buildings, temples, pottery and engravings. The pattern is repeated through a series of twists and turns, and in doing so resembles a key. This distinctive pattern is also known as the symbol of eternity. It is used in jewellery design, decorative arts, books, furniture and motifs. This pattern is also seen around the top edge of pottery, and other ceramic or metal décor items forming a decorative band. Often seen in architectural friezes, the Greek key provides at once a classical feel and distinctive look to buildings, decor and furniture.

Komboloi

Greek worry beads

Most Greek homes have Komboloi, also known as worry beads, placed on coffee tables, adorning sideboards or hung as decorative ornaments on walls. They are used widely throughout Greece and by Greek people worldwide, and are a popular memento from travels in Greece. The beads, which are used mostly by men, are a way to relax and relieve stress and to allow one to become present in the moment. Usually the beads are used almost meditatively to distract and still the mind from trouble and worry, or simply to allow reflection and contemplation.

Worry beads are colourful and smooth and are assembled on a long string. There are usually 20 beads on a looped string, followed by a knot with a couple more beads. Decorative tassels are attached to adorn the end of the komboloi.

Komboloi can be strung on fine metal chains, leather or string and come in a range of colours, sizes and ornamentation.

The usual method of handling the beads is to start by using the index finger and thumb to move the string forward until the last bead is reached. The cord is tipped, and then the beads fall. This is repeated until all the beads have fallen.

Alternatively, the beads can be hand rolled against each other, to create a soft 'click' sound, or flicked over one's hand whilst holding the beads between the thumb and pointer finger.

It is a very easy and quite relaxing pastime. Most Greek homes would have a collection of worry beads for decorative purposes as well as to use for relaxation.

A typical scene in Greece is one of men sitting at a kafeneion (coffee shop) sipping their coffee or taking an ouzo with meze, whilst clicking the komboloi and perhaps playing Backgammon or discussing recent events, politics or the usual philosophizing.

Greek Words

There are certain words in the Greek language that are used freely, however they don't really have a literal translation. Here are some of my favourites:

Meraki (pronounced meh-rah-kee)

This is often used to describe doing something with creativity, soul, or love; when you put something of yourself into what you're doing. This could involve cooking a meal, entertaining, decorating a room, setting a table, arranging flowers, or the work done in your garden. It's when you have passion about what you do and it's evident in the result.

Kefi (pronounced ke-fee)

This word is used when excitement, enthusiasm, high spirits and exuberance are experienced. It can be used to describe the atmosphere of a party or gathering; "It was a great night with lots of kefi". Usually this would mean that dancing, frivolity and fun were enjoyed by all, and not just some.

Opa! (pronounced oa-pah)

This word is used when one is experiencing kefi; feeling uplifted and enjoying the present moment. It is mostly used when one is dancing and very much into giving of themselves to the moment.

Opa can also be used to utter "stop" or "oopsy", or could be said if a child stumbles when learning to walk. Opa la!

Manari mou (pronounced ma-na-ree mou)

This is a term of endearment for a beautiful person, or used to address 'my love', or 'precious'. Mana mou is a shortened version and is also commonly used. But don't be confused with the word Mana, which literally means mother.

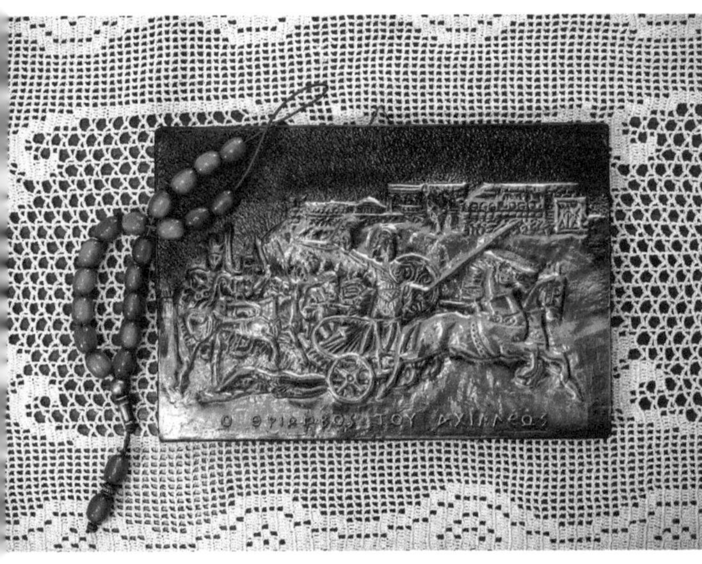
Ο ΘΡΙΑΜΒΟΣ ΤΟΥ ΑΧΙΛΛΕΩΣ

Ancient Greek Gods

Aphrodite:	Goddess of love, beauty, desire and pleasure
Apollo:	God of music, arts, light, knowledge and healing
Ares:	God of war
Artemis:	Goddess of the hunt, wilderness and animals
Athena:	Goddess of intelligence, warfare, strategy and wisdom
Demeter:	Goddess of grain, agriculture and harvest
Dionysus:	God of wine, parties and festivals
Hades:	King of the underworld
Hephaestus:	God of volcanoes, fire, metalworking and crafts
Hera:	Queen of the heavens and goddess of marriage, women, and childbirth
Hermes:	Olympian god of diplomacy, writing, language and communication
Hestia:	Goddess of the hearth, home and chastity
Poseidon:	God of the sea
Zeus:	King of the gods, ruler of Mount Olympus, god of the sky, weather, law, order and fate
Nike:	Winged goddess of victory

Αα Alpha	Ββ Beta	Γγ Gamma	Δδ Delta
Εε Epsilon	Ζζ Zeta	Ηη Eta	Θθ Theta
Ιι Iota	Κκ Kappa	Λλ Lambda	Μμ Mi
Νν Ni	Χχ Hi	Οο Omikron	Ππ Pi
Ρρ Rho	Σσς Sigma	Ττ Tuf	Υυ Ipsilon
Φφ Phi	Χχ Chi	Ψψ Psi	Ωω Omega

φιλοσοφια

Philosophy

"Philotimo to the Greek is like breathing. A Greek is not a Greek without it"

Thales

Acknowledgements
Αναγνώριση

Thank you to my parents for sharing the lessons. I was happy to learn, practice and pass forward the treasured traditions, and unique way in which our family practices our culture.

Thank you to my husband George who supported me whilst I sat at my computer turning my ideas and memories into this book. His feedback and insights are truly valued and have helped me refine the book throughout its journey. He is the man with whom I share my dreams.

Thank you to my three daughters Anna, Mary and Helena for their support in patiently listening to the progress updates, providing valuable feedback as well as igniting my energy and enthusiasm to keep going. Thank you for sharing in the excitement.

Thank you to my family members and friends who allowed me to share my thoughts and ideas with them and who took the time to provide honest feedback, shared enthusiasm and much valued help. You know who you are.

Very much like the literary figures of the 1920's who met at cafes in Paris to write, exchange ideas and pursue their dreams, my journey has been dotted with chance introductions and scheduled meetings at cafes both in the suburbs and the city that provided a perfect place for shared creativity and inspiration.

Thank you to my editor Melissa Sheldrick who was enthused by the idea for this book. Your wonderful energy and wealth of experience provided me with much enthusiasm and encouragement and a renewed belief in my journey, especially when I was feeling a little uncertain. The attention to detail and delicate handling of the text has shown an immense respect for the vision of this book that has now been enlivened with your valued contribution, whilst maintaining the integrity of my voice. Our serendipitous meeting at a café in Norwood has turned into a happy working relationship and wonderful friendship too.

Thank you to Steve Grice whom I met through Melissa. You listened carefully to my thoughts about the book and then sensitively and respectfully embraced my vision bringing to fruition a book that I'm so very proud of. Your feedback, insights and experience are truly valued as is your sincere demeanour and professionalism.

Styling and Photography

Thank you to my niece Marie Kargiotis who added her special talents in styling some of the images contained within the pages of this book, and for providing heartfelt feedback.

Thank you to Zoe Coates for photographing some of the images contained within these pages. Her photographic talents helped bring this book to life.

Support Team

Thank you to Father Kon Skoumbourdis from St George Greek Orthodox Church, Thebarton for taking the time to ensure that the religious content has indeed been included correctly. Your patience, feedback, and generosity of spirit, is truly and sincerely appreciated.

Thank you to J Andrew Johnstone whom I met serendipitously at a café in Norwood when his little daughter made her way towards my table. This chance encounter provided an opportunity for me to meet someone who had already travelled the road that I was on. Your insights, feedback and enthusiasm has helped me greatly and provided me with the confidence to give it a go. I thank you for your friendship.

Thank you to all those with whom I shared my passion about writing this book, and who gave me the much needed feedback and little nudges to push me forward gently and to eventually bring this book to fruition. I am grateful to everyone that has inspired and assisted me in some way.

Sincerely, thank you!
Σε ευχαριστουμε!

Eugenia

Greek Calendar

January	New Year's Day	038
	New Year Song	040
	Vasilopita Bread	042
	Vasilopita Cake	043
	Loukoumathes	044
	Epiphany - Holy Theophany	047
	Feast Day of St John	048
March	Evangelismos	052
	Greek Independence Day	052
	Secret School	054
	Masquerade (Apokries)	056
	Clean Monday	058
	Lagana Bread	060
	Fasting and Lent	062
	Fasting Recipes - Savoury	065
	Fasting Recipes - Sweet	088
	Easter	092
	Koulourakia	104
	Red Dyed Eggs	106
	Tsoureki	111
	Roast Lamb	112
April	St. George	116
May	May Day	117
	Saturday of the Soul	116
	Pentecost	116
	All Saints Day	116
August	Panayias	118
October	Ohi Day	118
December	Christmas	120
	Kourambiedes	122
	Melamakarona	124
	Finikia	126

Love and Other Ceremonies

Loggo -The Promise 128
Engagement 130
Krevati (dressing of the bed) 132
Dowry – Prika – Trousseau 134
Wedding preparation 134
Best Man/Matron of Honour 135
Wedding Service 137
Wedding song 140
Wedding Bread - Ioanian 143
Wedding Bread – Easy 144
Diples 146

Births and Baptism

Births 150
Sarantisi Blessing 150
Nursery Rhymes 151
Lullaby 151
Baptism 154
Nameday Celebrations 157

Death and Mourning

Offers of Help 164
Mourning 164
Trisagion (Last Rites) 165
Funeral and Burial 165
Memory Eternal 166
Expressions of Sympathy 166
Wake 169
Memorial Services 170
At the Cemetery 172
Sunday Memorial Service 173
Prosforo Bread 175
Artos Bread 176
Kolliva 178
Icon Stands 182
Kandilli Lamps 182
Incense Burner 184

Entertaining

The Greek Hostess 187
Kerasma 189
Philoxenia 189
Ouzo and mezze 192
Greek coffee 195
Spoon sweets 197
Vanilla Fondant 200

Kitchen Garden

Seasonal Gardening 204
Greek Cookery 206
Herbal Tea 208
Herbs 212
Spices 215
Riganada 219
Hilopites 221
Trahana – Sweet 222
Trahana – Sour 223
Pigeon Ragout 224
Olive Oil 227
Olives - Dried 228
Olives - in Brine 230
Wine 232
Cheese 235
Honey 235
Mastic 235

Greek Way of Life

When a child loses their baby teeth 252
On the occasion of buying something new 252
Greek Key 254
Worry Beads (komboloi) 254
Greek words 255
Ancient Greek Gods 258
Greek Alphabet 258

Recipes Index

Aginares me Arakas -
Artichokes with Peas 078
Artos Bread 176

Bakaliaros – Fried Salted Cod 079
Briami – Baked Vegetables 076

Cumquat Spoon Sweet 199

Diples 146

Fakes - Lentil Soup 065
Fasolatha - White Bean Soup 069
Fava Soup – Split Pea Soup 066
Fanouropita – Spicy Lenten Cake 237
Fassolakia Ladera – Green Bean Stew 077
Finikia –Spice Filled Biscuits 126

Greek Coffee 195
Galatopita – Baked Milk Pudding 245
Grape Spoon Sweet 198

Halva – Semolina Cake 090
Herbal Teas 208
Herbs 212
Hilopites – Home-made Egg Pasta 221
Horta – Boiled Greens 084

Kalamaraki – Fried Calamari 071
Kolliva – Boiled Wheat with Spices 178
Koulourakia – Easter Biscuits 104

Kourambiedes – Almond Shortbread 122
Lagana Bread 060
Lamb, Roast 112

Lenten Cake 088
Loukoumathes – Honey Donoughts 044

Melamakarona –
Honey and Walnut Biscuits 124
Moustalevria – Grape Juice Pudding 241
Moustokouloura – Grape Must Biscuits 089

Olives in Brine 230
Olives – Dried 228

Pantzaria – Beetroot 082
Petemezi- Grape Must Syrup 242
Pigeon Ragout 224
Prawn Saganaki 073
Prosforo Bread 175

Quince Spoon Sweet 200

Ravani tou Mourias –
Baked Semolina Cake 243
Red Dyed Eggs – Simple 108
Red Dyed Eggs – Decorated 109
Revithia – Chickpea Soup 068
Riganada – Tomato on Bread 219
Rizogalo – rice pudding 239

Skordalia – Garlic Sauce 081
Spanakorizo – Spinach Rice 070
Spices 215
Spoon Sweet 197
Tarama – Fish Roe Dip 087
Tomato Salsa 072
Trahana – Sour 223
Trahana – Sweet 222
Tsoureki – Easter Bread 111

Vanilla Fondant 200
Vasilopita – New Year Bread 042
Vasilopita – New Year Cake 043

Wedding Bread – Ionian 143
Wedding Bread – Easy 144

Yoghurt 247

Zoe Coates

Front cover, pages 36, 74, 75, 80, 83, 86, 114, 115, 123, 125, 131, 133,136, 141, 148, 158, 159, 160, 177, 183, 186, 188, 190, 193, 194, 196, 201, 207, 210, 211, 218, 229, 233, 234, 249, 250

Page 168 (top right image of bread stamp

Page 168 (middle right image of candle)

Page 225 (top right image of olive oils)

Page 225 (top left image of mortar & pestle)

Page 225 (bottom left image of wine)

Page 248 (except top right image of anchor – author's own)

Page 256 (except top left image of garden statue – author's own)

Page 256 (except bottom left image of spoons in glass – author's own)

Page 257 (except top right image of demitasse cups – author's own)

Marie Kargiotis

Page 94 (red eggs on lawn, red eggs with bougainvillea)

Family Archives

Page 15, 19, 20, 22

Anna Pantahos

Page 167, Priest, George and Eugenia with incense burner at my mother's memorial service.

Page 168, top left (incense burner), bottom left (kolliva), and bottom right (bread)

Mary Pantahos

Page 256, bottom left - Grapes in cup

Eugenia Pantahos

All other images and all other props are author's own.

Michael Reed

Page 46, bottom right – Blessing of the Water, Glenelg Beach, South Australia.

Props provided by Lavina Desyllas

Page 36, Statue of discus thrower, and teal and cream tin. Page 248, bottom left (Greek national costume dolls), Page 249, top right (Greek cap), middle right (large pomegranate) bottom left (Greek pottery), and Page 250 (colourful plate).

Props provided by my father, John Desyllas

Page 257, middle right (copper urns), bottom left (Greek national costume dolls), and bottom right (collection of painted copper plates).